Manual on
Tourism and Poverty Alleviation
Practical Steps for Destinations

Manual on Tourism and Poverty Alleviation – Practical Steps for Destinations
ISBN: 978-92-844-1343-0 (UNWTO)
ISBN: 978-9077821305 (SNV)

Published by the World Tourism Organization and the Netherlands Development Organization
Printed by the World Tourism Organization, Madrid, Spain
First printing 2010
All rights reserved

World Tourism Organization
Calle Capitán Haya, 42
28020 Madrid, Spain
Tel.: (+34) 915 678 100
Fax: (+34) 915 713 733
Website: www.unwto.org
Email: omt@unwto.org

SNV Netherlands Development Organization
Dr. Kuyperstraat 5
2514 BA The Hague, Netherlands
Tel.: (+31) (0)70 344 0244
Fax: (+31) (0)70 385 5531
Website: www.snvworld.org
Email: info@snvworld.org

Table of Contents

Foreword by the World Tourism Organization

Tourism's development in the last decades has been extraordinary when compared with several other sectors, and developing countries have benefitted from higher growth rates. Since 1990, international tourism receipts in developing countries have increased by a factor of six while high-income countries have registered a twofold increase. However, the concept of tourism as a tool for development and for poverty alleviation is recent and needs to be consolidated and to gain recognition and acceptance. The ST-EP programme was initially conceived by the UNWTO as a practical application of the notion of tourism constituting a powerful tool for development, as stated in the 2002 Johannesburg Plan of Implementation. Since then much progress has been achieved with an increasing number of projects already concluded and many others being implemented in a wide range of developing countries.

The UNWTO could not have made such remarkable advances without the support of several partners. SNV stands out for having engaged side by side with us, enriching the ST-EP programme with its professionalism, enthusiasm and thorough knowledge of several countries where we are working together. The joint initiative of preparing this manual is a further token of our outstanding cooperation.

In order to benefit the poorer segments of countries and communities, tourism development needs to be guided by a solid methodology, translating the seven mechanisms for poverty reduction into a clear and accessible manual addressed to a wide range of stakeholders. This is the aim of this work which we hope will become a reference and a tool for capacity building for the next generation of ST-EP projects and a contribution toward mainstreaming poverty reduction approaches in all tourism strategies. We also believe that it will facilitate the development of the tourism potential that is still largely unharnessed in favour of economic and social growth in developing countries.

Luigi Cabrini
Director, Sustainable Development of Tourism Programme
World Tourism Organization

Foreword by the Netherlands Development Organisation – SNV

SNV Netherlands Development Organisation has been supporting sustainable tourism development since the early 1990s, recognizing the significance of the sector for developing economies and its potential as a tool for poverty reduction. Currently, SNV supports tourism programmes in 25 of the 33 countries in which it works, in Africa, Asia, the Balkans and Latin America. SNV employs two interrelated approaches to guide its interventions – destination development and private sector engagement – and this manual is a valuable tool to assist practitioners to support the private sector, NGOs and local governments with inclusive tourism destination development.

In November 2004, SNV and UNWTO signed partnership agreements to fund and support Technical Assistance for Sustainable Tourism – Eliminating Poverty (ST-EP). In its first phase, the partnership supported 23 projects on policy and strategy formulation, projects addressing the seven UNWTO-proposed poverty reduction mechanisms, and knowledge development and management activities. Together with the ST-EP Foundation a second phase of the partnership started in 2007, supporting 21 larger ST-EP project packages based on the seven poverty reduction mechanisms. These seven mechanisms have become an international reference for many tourism and development organisations. The experience amassed through the formulation and implementation of ST-EP projects in different developing countries has indicated the need to share experiences and build capacities on tools and methodologies to apply the mechanisms.

These efforts have a special relevance to the UNWTO/ST-EP Foundation/SNV partnership, which extends beyond the delivery of ST-EP projects. This manual brings together the extensive expertise developed within the respective agencies in this field to advance practical, pro-poor tourism methodologies for a broader audience, as well as support the implementation of ongoing ST-EP projects.

Paul Stevens

Senior Advisor / Corporate Network Leader
Pro-Poor Sustainable Tourism
SNV Netherlands Development Organisation

Acknowledgements

This publication has been prepared for the World Tourism Organization (UNWTO) and SNV Netherlands Development Organisation by Richard and Jackie Denman of The Tourism Company, UK based tourism consultants. It draws on a range material referenced in the publication.

The final version of the *Manual on Tourism and Poverty Alleviation – Practical Steps for Destinations* is a collaborative effort of UNWTO and SNV.

Thanks are due, particularly, to staff of UNWTO and SNV advisers of Africa, Asia, the Balkans and Latin America. The development of the manual was initiated and first coordinated by Gabor Vereczi, then Chief, Environment and Quality Section, UNWTO, John Hummel, Pro-Poor Sustainable Tourism Network leader SNV Asia, and Anna Spenceley, former SNV Senior Tourism Advisor.

The final review, editing and coordination of this publication were done by Tara Gujadhur of SNV and Marcel Leijzer, Deputy Director Development Assistance Programme, Luigi Cabrini, Director Sustainable Development of Tourism Programme (SDT), and Sofía Gutiérrez, Programme Officer SDT, of UNWTO.

About this Manual

Tourism is one of the strongest drivers of world trade and prosperity. Poverty alleviation is one of the greatest global challenges. Despite turbulent times for the world's economy, these basic facts are unlikely to change. Focusing the wealth creating power of tourism on people most in need remains an immense task and opportunity.

Much has been written in the past ten years on the link between tourism and poverty alleviation. We understand more about it now. Yet more has been written about the theory than the practice.

The purpose of this manual is to outline some practical steps, in simple language, that can be taken in tourism destinations to shape and manage tourism in ways which deliver more benefits to disadvantaged individuals and communities. It is not a general guide to tourism development but focuses on how to channel tourism income more effectively to the poor.

The manual is aimed at organizations and individuals working in the field of tourism at the destination level, or those working more widely at this level to support poverty alleviation with an interest in seeing how tourism development and management can help and how they can assist with this. A primary audience is seen as local government officials, but the manual is also intended for people working in other public sector agencies, NGOs and advisory bodies. More broadly, in showing how they can support poverty alleviation in tourism destinations, it is also relevant to governments at a national level, to the private sector, and to international development agencies.

The manual is in three main parts, based on the three classic components of a project cycle: Analysis/Planning, Action and Assessment.

PART 1 covers analysis and planning. It shows how to take poverty alleviation into account in considering stakeholders and beneficiaries, analysing the current performance of tourism, considering future potential and developing a strategy and action plan.

PART 2 covers action. It provides details on practical ways of delivering tourism benefits to the poor, based on seven mechanisms previously identified by UNWTO. These include: direct employment; supply chains; informal selling; enterprise development; taxes and charges; voluntary giving; and collateral benefits.

PART 3 covers assessment. It looks at the use of indicators and measurement processes to evaluate the impact of tourism and individual initiatives on poverty.

The manual can be used:

- As a stand alone **advisory publication** and **reference source.**

- To prompt **thought and response.** At the end of each section are boxes which invite the reader to think about how the content applies to his/her own destination.

- To support short **training programmes.** A suggestion for a possible programme is provided in Annex 5.

Introduction

Context and Principles

This introductory section shows how the manual relates to international interest in tourism and poverty alleviation and to the work of UNWTO and SNV. It explains the special position of tourism as a tool in tackling poverty and underlines that this should be an objective for all tourism based on some basic principles.

UNWTO and SNV – Working together and with others

The link between tourism and poverty alleviation was recognised by the UN back in 1999, when the Commission on Sustainable Development (CSD 7) urged governments to "maximise the potential of tourism for eradicating poverty by developing appropriate strategies in co-operation with all major groups and local communities." This was further endorsed by the Plan of Implementation of the World Summit on Sustainable Development (WSSD) in Johannesburg in 2002, which was the first time that the output from such an event had specifically included an article on tourism as a tool for poverty alleviation.

Since that time, The World Tourism Organization (UNWTO) has promoted poverty alleviation as a major objective of sustainable tourism development and of its own work in this field. It has published various studies on the subject, to guide its work and that of others, which are included as references. A major initiative was the establishment of the Sustainable Tourism – Elimination of Poverty (ST-EP) Programme, which was launched by UNWTO in 2002 at the WSSD. The Government of the Republic of Korea was a pioneer partner in the launching of the ST-EP Programme by offering an initial contribution of US$ 5 million to host and establish a ST-EP Foundation in Seoul. In addition, a number of other donors and development organizations have offered financial and technical support to the ST-EP Programme, including contributions from SNV Netherlands Development Organisation, the Italian Government, the French Government, the Spanish Development Agency AECID, the Ramsar Convention Secretariat, the Government of Macao SAR, the Flemish Government, the Korean International Cooperation Agency (KOICA), the Tsingtao Brewery Company, and IUCN the Netherlands. With the support from these various sources, between 2005 and 2009, some 90 projects in 31 countries have been supported by the programme. This manual is partly based on experience gained from these projects and, in turn, will provide a learning resource and training material for use within the programme in future.

SNV Netherlands Development Organisation has been involved with tourism since 1994, and currently works in 20 countries in five regions of the world developing sustainable tourism activities. It is in a formal partnership with UNWTO and the ST-EP Programme and has supported the latter from the beginning with finance and technical assistance. SNV works to realize poverty reduction through increasing the production, income and employment opportunities for the poor, and builds the capacity of local organizations and actors to do this through tourism. In the last five years it has commissioned a number of studies on how financial flows in the tourism sector reach the poor, together with other technical and advisory reports based on SNV's significant field experience in this sector. Again, they are referenced in the bibliography, p. 111. This manual draws on them and converts their findings into practical action steps.

In recent years tourism has received more attention from many different agencies working to alleviate poverty. The World Bank and regional development banks, for example, have included tourism initiatives in their focus on sustainable development in a number of countries. UNWTO and SNV work in partnership with many other development assistance agencies on tourism and poverty alleviation projects, as well as with governments and the private sector, including the supporters of the ST-EP Programme mentioned above. This manual is seen as relevant to all of them.

Tourism's special position in poverty alleviation

Why should we pay particular attention to tourism in the fight against poverty? Three key reasons are given below.

1.   The relative importance of tourism in developing countries.

In many developing countries, but not all, tourism is already a major player in the economy. Here are some facts:[1]

– International tourism receipts by developing countries amounted to over US$ 259 billion in 2007.

– Tourism is the primary source of foreign earnings for the world's 49 Least Developed Countries.[2]

– Tourism is a principal export in over 80% of developing countries and the main export of one third of them.

– In some developing countries, notably small island states, tourism can account for over 25% of GDP.

2.   The size and growth of the sector.

In 2008, international tourist arrivals stood at 922 million, generating some US$ 944 billion in receipts. In the five previous years, annual growth had averaged 4% but was considerably faster among developing countries. While a static or declining picture is forecast for 2009 and 2010, the UNWTO still predicts 1.6 billion international tourist arrivals by 2020. Domestic tourism (travel within the country by residents) has also been growing significantly in many developing countries and this will continue.

3.   The character of tourism.

There are many characteristics of tourism as an activity which make it particularly relevant to low income countries and to poor communities within them. These include:

– **Its response to particular assets.** Tourism places great value on some common features of developing countries, such as warm climate, rich cultural heritage, inspiring landscapes and abundant biodiversity. These strengths can be particularly apparent in rural areas, which may have a comparative advantage for tourism while being at a disadvantage in most other economic sectors.

– **Its accessibility to the poor.** Tourism is a relatively labour intensive sector and is traditionally made up of small and micro enterprises. Many activities in tourism are particularly suited to women, young people and disadvantaged groups such as ethnic minority populations. Many tourism jobs are potentially quite accessible to the poor as they require relatively few skills and little investment. Some may also be part time and used to supplement income from other activities.

– **Its connectivity.** As so many different activities and inputs make up the tourism product, spending by tourists can benefit a wide range of sectors such as agriculture, handicrafts, transport and other services. Additional rounds of spending by those people whose income is supported by tourism spread the economic benefit further (the multiplier effect).

---

1   Mainly taken from World Tourism Organization, 2004b.

2   Excluding oil which, although the largest contributor overall, is only relevant to three countries.

- **Its linking of consumers to producers.** Tourism, unusually, is an activity which brings the consumers to the producers. The interaction between tourists and poor communities can provide a number of intangible and practical benefits. These can range from increased awareness of cultural, environmental, and economic issues and values, on both sides, to mutual benefits from improved local investment in infrastructure.

On the other hand, there are also negative aspects of tourism as a basis for poverty alleviation, which require particular attention to the way it is managed. The main ones include:

- **Unpredictability and fluctuations in demand.** Tourism is very sensitive to economic, environmental, and socio-political events affecting tourists' willingness to travel. In the absence of insurance cover and social security, the poor can be particularly vulnerable to sudden downswings in demand. However, tourism demand often bounces back quickly when circumstances change.

- **The seasonal nature of demand** which can be very peaked. This requires good integration between tourism and other economic activities to provide a sufficient year-round source of livelihood.

- **Impact on life-supporting resources.** These include water, land, food, energy sources and biodiversity. Their availability to the poor can be threatened by competition and over use from tourism. Degradation of cultural assets and disruption to social structures are parallel threats. Global issues of resource depletion and environmental degradation may be as important as local ones, including the long term effect of tourism on climate change and the impact of adaptation and mitigation measures on travel patterns.

- **Weak linkages to the poor.** The nature of tourism investment and lack of engagement of the poor can cause much tourism spending to leak away from poor destinations. The income that remains may not end up benefiting the poor, reaching instead the better educated and well-off segments of society.

Tourism should not be seen on its own as 'the answer' to the elimination of poverty but it can make a powerful contribution. The potential to develop more tourism and to channel a higher percentage of tourism spending towards the poor may be great in some areas and quite small in others. However, given the size of the sector, even small changes in approach when widely applied can make a significant difference.

A mainstreamed but focussed approach

Many initiatives and projects that have sought to use tourism to tackle poverty have been criticised as being too narrow, lacking in commercial realism, small scale and achieving little overall impact on poverty.[3] Many have been informed only by local needs rather than by market potential and have not been viable or economically sustainable. There has been a tendency to equate a poverty-focussed approach to tourism with relatively narrow concepts such as 'community-based tourism' and 'ecotourism'.

The term 'pro-poor' is used throughout this manual to mean favouring the poor [4]. The term 'pro-poor tourism' (PPT) has been used as shorthand for tourism that results in increased net benefits for poor people.[5] It has always been emphasised that pro-poor tourism is not a specific product or niche sector but an approach to tourism development and management. Yet the term 'pro-poor tourism' has sometimes

---

3   Scheyvens, 2007.

4   The World Bank states that growth which is pro-poor is about "changing the distribution of relative incomes through the growth process to favour the poor" (from www.worldbank.org (1-11-2009) in 2009).

5   Pro-Poor Tourism Partnership. The Partnership has pioneered work on tourism and poverty alleviation and a wealth of information is available on the website www.propoortourism.org.uk (1-11-2009).

been misconstrued as narrowing the type of tourism under consideration rather than its impact, as so often is the case when an adjective is placed before the word tourism. For this reason this term is used guardedly in this manual and strictly in the wider sense of the above definition.

The need to work with the mainstream, to influence the tourism sector as a whole, is fully accepted. Studies have confirmed the need for this if a significant volumetric change is to be made to poverty.[6]

Given an overall aim of increasing the amount of economic and other benefits gained by the poor, the approach should be twofold:

A)   To increase the size and performance of the tourism sector as a whole (size of the cake) – through increasing, for example, the number of visits, length of stay and spend per person.

B)   To increase the proportion of spending in the sector that reaches the poor (share of the cake) – through specific action to enable and help the poor participate in tourism or benefit from it indirectly.

Figure 1   The size and share of the cake

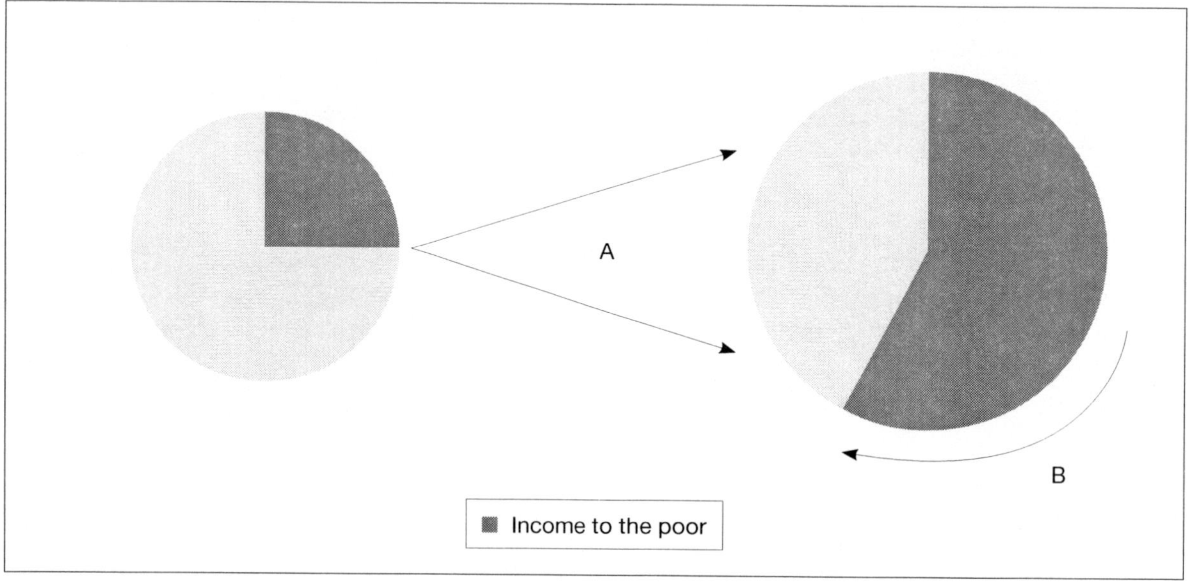

This manual focuses in particular on objective B.

Working in the mainstream of tourism will require an emphasis on two key challenges:

* Engaging private sector businesses, including sizeable operations and investors as well as small and micro businesses. This is where tourism wealth is created and distributed. They should be helped to deliver more benefits to the poor, through employment practices, local linkages and pro-poor tourism activities and products, as well as to be more competitive.

* Ensuring that tourism destinations as a whole are both competitive and sustainable, addressing issues of resource management and the relationship between tourism and other economic sectors.

This does not mean that one should move away entirely from working at a very local level within communities. This may well be required in order to engage with and reach the poor, to fully understand and address their needs, and to create opportunities accessible to them. This must, however, relate properly to the wider tourism context and the market.

The approach put forward here and followed in the remainder of this manual is therefore centred on sound destination management. It is based on structures that involve businesses of all kinds, together

____

6   Ashley and Goodwin, 2007.

with the public sector and civil society, and which have a commitment to poverty alleviation as a key aim. Some principles behind this approach are presented in box 1.

Box 1 10 Principles for pursuing poverty alleviation through tourism[7]

1 All aspects and types of tourism can and should be concerned about poverty alleviation.

2 All governments should include poverty alleviation as a key aim of tourism development and consider tourism as a possible tool for alleviating poverty.

3 The competitiveness and economic success of tourism businesses and destinations is critical to poverty alleviation – without this the poor cannot benefit.

4 All tourism businesses should be concerned about the impact of their activities on local communities and seek to benefit the poor through their actions.

5 Tourism destinations should be managed with poverty alleviation as a central aim that is built into strategies and action plans.

6 A sound understanding of how tourism functions in destinations is required, including how tourism income is distributed and who benefits from this.

7 Planning and development of tourism in destinations should involve a wide range of interests, including participation and representation from poor communities.

8 All potential impacts of tourism on the livelihood of local communities should be considered, including current and future local and global impacts on natural and cultural resources.

9 Attention must be paid to the viability of all projects involving the poor, ensuring access to markets and maximising opportunities for beneficial links with established enterprises.

10 Impacts of tourism on poverty alleviation should be effectively monitored.

---

7 These principles acknowledge and have taken account of previous, longstanding and highly relevant principles for 'pro-poor tourism' (e.g. Ashley et al (2000); Pro-Poor Tourism Partnership (2005)).

Part 1

Analysis and Planning –
Destination Management for Poverty Alleviation

This part of the manual looks at the process of analysing a tourism destination in terms of the current contribution of tourism to the poor and planning how this can be strengthened in future.

It is set in the context of **destination management,** which has been defined as the co-ordinated management of all the elements that make up a destination, taking a strategic approach.[1] Destination management embraces a whole range of activities including planning, promoting and controlling tourism development, providing and managing relevant infrastructure, supporting tourism enterprises, marketing the destination and providing visitor information, and managing the impacts of tourism on the environment and local residents. Fundamentally, this manual does not attempt to provide comprehensive guidance on the individual elements of destination management, such as how to market a destination, which would go way beyond its scope and purpose. Such guidance is available elsewhere.[2] Rather, it concentrates on analysis and planning to deliver a pro-poor orientation to destination management.

Identifying the destination as the basis for working

At the outset, and irrespective of pro-poor considerations, it is important to identify the destination geographically.

A **tourism destination** has been defined as:[3]

> *"A physical space in which a tourist spends at least one overnight. It includes tourism products such as support services and attractions and tourist resources within one day's return travel time. It has physical and administrative boundaries defining its management, and images and perceptions defining its market competitiveness. Local destinations incorporate various stakeholders often including a host community, and can nest and network to form larger destinations".*

Based on this definition, destinations can vary considerably in size. They could be whole countries, regions, districts, cities, towns or individual villages. However, for the destination management process to be effective and efficient, a destination should comply with the following criteria:

- can be clearly defined, through existing boundaries or physical features;

- has some strong features and characteristics that enables it to be recognised by tourists and promoted to them as a specific area to visit;

- contains a range of assets and enterprises sufficient to attract tourists and support a local tourism industry;

- has sufficient appeal to be realistically promoted independently in certain markets;

- relates to local governance structures and existing or potential stakeholder structures who can engage in destination management;

- is large enough, in terms of population and (potential) volume of tourism, to justify and support its own destination management activity;

---

1   Paraphrased from World Tourism Organization, 2007.
2   Ibid.
3   Ibid.

- is small enough to enable effective communication between all stakeholders and engender a commitment between them to work together.

Typically, effective destinations that meet these criteria will be small regions, provinces, districts, cities, sizeable resort towns or clearly definable rural areas. They could also be defined by natural or cultural assets, such as national parks or major heritage sites and the tourism infrastructure associated with them. They might be locations linked by a tourist circuit.

Although destination management should centre on the kinds of area described above, it may be appropriate for the planning and implementation of certain actions to occur at different levels – either smaller areas within the destination or larger areas that include the destination alongside others. In particular:

- Work may be carried out in specific towns or villages or with individual local or indigenous communities, to identify needs and opportunities and to develop products, within the context of the overall destination strategy.

- The destination may work with neighbouring destinations or with higher level regional or national authorities on activities such as marketing and setting standards.

A pro-poor approach to destination management

The sections on analysis and planning which follow contain seven steps or elements of destination management that are considered to be particularly relevant to a pro-poor approach. Within each, issues of particular relevance to poverty alleviation are identified and addressed.

The steps are as follows:

1   Ensuring supportive government policies.

2   Working effectively with different stakeholders.

3   Identifying who should benefit and their needs.

4   Understanding how tourism is working currently and who is benefiting.

5   Judging the destination's future potential for tourism that benefits the poor.

6   Agreeing on a strategy and action plan to alleviate poverty through tourism.

7   Strengthening stakeholder response and capacity.

The contents of part 2 of the manual, covering specific actions, and of part 3, covering assessment of impact, should be considered also as integral parts of destination management, even though they are presented separately in this manual.

NB:

- These steps do not need to be taken entirely sequentially. Some may involve work that is pursued throughout the process or is revisited from time to time.

- The work required for each step does not have to be complex or onerous. Some destinations may wish to move swiftly to taking specific actions and not use up limited resources on research and plans.[4] The steps could be taken by bringing together a few key people, asking a few basic questions and noting down key conclusions or they could involve more detailed research and analysis.

---

4   The example of Inhambane, Mozambique (box 8, p. 39) is relevant here.

1 Identifying your destination and steps taken and to take

1 Think of an area which you believe could be described as a tourist destination. This may be your own area.

– Does it meet the criteria identified above in terms of identity, size and the range of services available?

– How would you define the destination – what are its boundaries?

– Should it be linked to other areas for certain purposes?

– Are there distinctive smaller areas or communities within the destination that you may wish to work with?

2 Look at the seven steps set out on page 2.

– Are they all important to you?

– Have you taken some of them already?

1.1 Ensuring Supportive Government Policies

Despite the focus placed by this manual on analysis, planning and action at a destination level, the commitment of government, from the national level downwards, to tourism and to making it more pro-poor remains critically important. Indeed, the right government policies and legislation are essential to enable, support and give weight and legitimacy to action within destinations. This requires attention from various parts of government and their advisors. Stakeholders working within destinations should actively seek to influence national as well as local policies and also ensure that they are fully acquainted with them.

In most countries the key ministry will be the Ministry of Tourism (or the ministry containing tourism within its responsibilities). However, other ministries should recognise and support the role of tourism in poverty alleviation, notably those responsible for finance, development, trade, planning, agriculture, environment and natural resources, transport, security, education and culture. Awareness and co-ordination of ministries can be promoted through holding **inter-ministerial tourism forums** or other regular liaison mechanisms.

1.1.1 Securing Two-way Commitment to Poverty and Tourism

A fundamental requirement of government is that:

• policies aimed at poverty reduction should recognise the role of tourism and commit the government to tourism development that is pro-poor; and

• tourism policies should contain poverty alleviation as a major aim and outline actions relevant to achieving this.

Poverty Reduction Strategy Papers (PRSPs) enshrine the poverty alleviation policies in most developing countries. They describe a country's macroeconomic, structural and social policies and programs to promote growth and reduce poverty, as well as associated external financing needs. They are prepared by governments through a participatory process involving civil society and development partners, including the World Bank and the International Monetary Fund (IMF). Analysis in 2005 showed that

80% of PRSPs at that time made some reference to tourism.[5] However, this may just refer to tourism's contribution to macro economic growth and foreign exchange earnings, rather than setting out policy commitments.[6] It would be more helpful if the strategy committed the government to support more specific pro-poor actions for the tourism, such as building cross-sector linkages at a local level. PRSPs are not only key to securing pan-government support; they also have a major influence on the priorities of development assistance agencies in their allocation of funding within each country. Destinations can refer to PRSPs when approaching donors to seek funding for ST-EP projects in a destination.

National tourism strategies should not only recognise the potential for poverty alleviation, they should consider opportunities for benefitting the poor in the type and location of tourism development they call for and in their proposals for marketing, training and other support services. Good tourism strategies are clearly important in driving effective tourism marketing and development policies and actions for the country as a whole. However, they should also provide the lead for a pro-poor approach amongst the private sector, local government and other stakeholders. They can do this partly by underlining the strategic importance of small, medium and micro enterprises, public-private partnerships, linkages between different stakeholders, and collaboration processes. They can give legitimacy and weight to the concept of destination management, referred to at the end of this section.

Tourism laws should recognise poverty alleviation as a legitimate purpose for tourism development. Elements commonly covered by tourism laws, such as definitions, standards and requirements of accommodation facilities, tour operators and guides, should be written so that they recognise the special circumstances of micro and community based enterprises. Tourism laws can be used to provide legal backing for structures and interventions, such as accreditation schemes, regulated training provision, financial assistance and taxation regimes, that may be designed to support pro-poor development and sound operational practice. More specifically, tourism laws could contain elements to underpin specific and processes, such as enforcing public-private partnership contracts that have benefits for local people, and formalisation of the informal sector.

1.1.2 Influencing other Areas of Policy and Legislation

An enabling environment for pro-poor tourism will depend as much on national policies and legislation in other fields as on specific tourism or poverty alleviation policies. The following are of particular importance:

- **Labour laws.** These may cover terms and conditions for employees and statutory minimum wages. Clauses which legalise labour unions and prohibit discrimination on grounds of race, gender, religion and disability can be particularly relevant to the poor. Minimum age limits can help protect against misuse of child labour. Some countries have used legislation to support targets for employment of historically disadvantaged people. More specific legislation, for example on handling and dispersal of gratuities, can also be helpful.

- **Policies affecting physical planning, transport, environment and natural resources.** Through affecting the scale and location of development, ease of access and flow of tourists, they can have an indirect but critical effect on opportunities for poor communities in different locations to gain benefit. These policies and related legislation can also be used to control development which could lead to degradation of resources precious to poor communities. Policies relating to national parks and protected areas can directly affect whether the communities in and around them can benefit from tourism; while legislation on issues such as use of admission fees and leasing of concessions to the private sector (with contractual benefits to local people) can help to enable this. The processes by which the policies are made should also include a participatory approach, where the people who live in destinations can contribute in a meaningful way.

---

5   Mann, 2005.

6   Pro-Poor Tourism Partnership, 2004.

- **Policies and legislation relating to business development.** In addition to relevant specific provision in tourism laws, general policy and legislation governing business can also be important, for example covering business security, access to credit and the operation of public-private partnerships. An investment policy can provide incentives, such as tax exemption, to attract new investments generally or in poorer or more remote areas. In some countries, entrepreneurs have to meet certain conditions regarding local employment and locally purchasing goods and services, in order to qualify for these exemptions.

- **Legislation relating to land tenure and community rights.** Clarity and stability with respect to land tenure can be very important in enabling local people (individuals and communities) to benefit from tourism, for example through leasing out land for development. Some land tenure systems make this difficult (e.g. Rwanda, Mozambique); in others it is easier (e.g. Namibia, South Africa). Stable land tenure can benefit the private sector as well, removing uncertainties in their relationships with communities and removing a barrier to investment. Clarification of other community rights, for example with respect to ownership and protection of cultural assets and traditional knowledge, is also important.

Sometimes contradictions and inconsistencies are found between the different areas of policy and legislation that affect poverty alleviation through tourism; this should be checked and avoided.

1.1.3 Ensuring Effective Implementation

Relevant policy and supportive legislation are only part of the requirement. Too often, these have been in place but are not properly implemented. The chance of successful implementation can be increased by:

- Political backing for tourism and the relevant policies in the context of poverty alleviation. This can be helped through advocacy.

- Effective governance structures at a national and local level.

- Awareness of corruption and measure to ensure against it.

- Effective monitoring and reporting procedures.

The focus on destination level planning and management of tourism, promoted in this manual, can help in ensuring the implementation of policies and legislation on the ground.

1.1.4 Securing Government Backing for Destination Management and Local Action

Government policy and legislation should also support the actual process of destination management and provide a mandate for this. Tourism policies should set out the purpose and advantages of decentralisation and indicate the division of roles and responsibilities between national and local levels. This should be backed up by relevant allocation of budgets. Guidelines should be set on the required structures and processes within destinations. Poverty alleviation should be stipulated as an aim of destination management.

In some countries, the spatial framework for destination management may be determined centrally, for example through the designation of tourism development or management areas. This can be helpful in focussing effort on areas with particular tourism potential, but at the same time such designation should take account of priority areas for the alleviation of poverty. Local governance structures should also be fully taken into account in such designations so that resulting initiatives work with or within them rather than across them.

Box 2 Enabling policies in South Africa[7]

In South Africa the direction of tourism development towards an approach which is sustainable and pro-poor was set by the government's White Paper on the Development and Promotion of Tourism in 1996. This reflected widespread consultation country-wide which revealed considerable concern amongst local communities about their involvement in tourism. Policies stemming from the White Paper have supported tools to encourage and incentivise the private sector to address poverty issues and to strengthen linkages with communities, whose engagement in tourism is also supported. Examples include a Tourism Public-Private Partnership Toolkit and the legislation and institutional strengthening to support skills development and acquisition of qualifications in the sector by disadvantaged people.

The White Paper has not only affected national policy. Guidelines for Responsible Tourism, stemming from the White Paper were drawn up, with all the Provinces involved in this. Subsequently, the Provinces have developed policies and planning frameworks which reflect these principles. More locally, Destination Management Organizations have been established around tourism nodes, and integrated approaches to tourism have been pursued in many national parks and conservation areas.

Wider supportive legislation in South Africa includes the Broad Based Black Economic Empowerment (BBBEE) Act, 2003. This set targets, monitored through a scorecard, for enterprises to benefit historically disadvantaged people, many of whom are poor. Criteria are: levels of their involvement in ownership, management, employment, and training within the enterprise; procurement from BBBEE suppliers; and support for community projects.

Specific national polices and legislation to increase the chances of poor communities benefiting from tourism included changes in the policy base of South Africa National Parks (a parastatal body) to enable public-private partnerships to work in national parks – see box 9.

 **1.1 Considering the government policy framework**

1 Think about the attention paid to the relationship between tourism and poverty alleviation at a national level in your country.

 – List the Ministries that you think have a role to play in this. Do they get together to discuss tourism and coordinate policy and action?

 – Does the Poverty Reduction Strategy refer adequately to tourism?

 – Is there a National Tourism Strategy? Is poverty alleviation recognised as a key objective, with relevant actions?

2 Consider which laws in your country are relevant to enabling the poor to benefit from tourism.

 – Do you know enough about them?

 – Do you think that they may need strengthening?

3 Is the relevant national policy framework and legislation working? What are the main problems with implementation?

---

4 Consider the decentralisation of policies and action to support tourism development and management in your country.

- Is this encouraged and supported by national policy?

- To what extent are local government structures encouraged and resourced to support tourism?

- Have specific destination management areas been identified and would this be helpful?

1.2 Working Effectively with Different Stakeholders

A central requirement of good destination management is for the process to involve a full range of stakeholders,[8] who feel engaged and are enabled to work together. This is particularly important if poverty alleviation objectives are to be fully understood and addressed.

In a typical destination a large number of different types of stakeholder can be identified, who can influence tourism or are affected by it. They include public sector organizations, private sector enterprises, civil society bodies, households and individuals. Some key stakeholders are illustrated in figure 2.

Figure 2   The spread of stakeholders

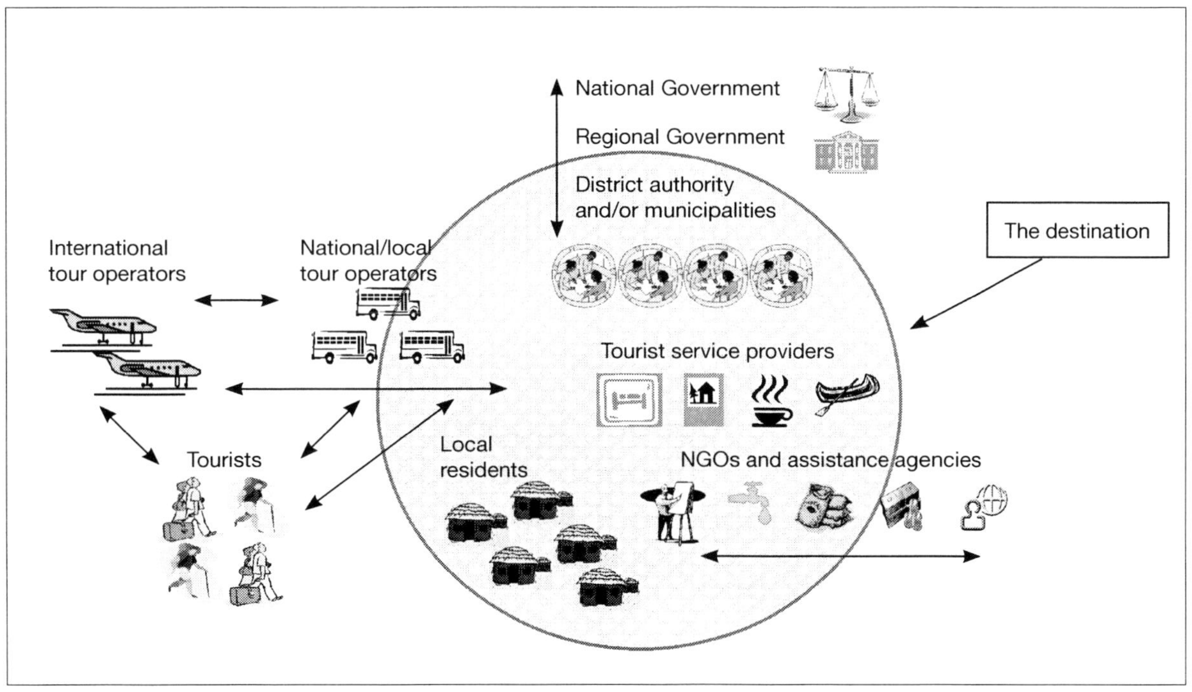

8   A 'stakeholder' has been defined as "any individual, community, group or organization with an interest in the outcome of an activity, either as a result of being affected by it or by being able to influence it." (Adapted from Department for International Development, 2002.)

1.2.1 Reflecting the Benefits and Obstacles to Collaboration

There are many compelling reasons why stakeholders should work together to deliver sustainable tourism which focuses on poverty alleviation. They include:

- **Promoting** – Raising and spreading awareness, support and commitment.

- **Sensitising** – Making sure different interests are understood and respected.

- **Coordinating** – Agreeing aims, aligning actions, filling gaps, avoiding duplication.

- **Learning** – Enhancing and exchanging knowledge and skills.

- **Sharing** – Pooling human, technical and financial resources and splitting costs.

- **Linking** – Joining together products, suppliers and markets.

However, the potential for effective collaboration and the best way to bring this about will vary between destinations. It is particularly important to be aware of the political and socio-cultural context in each case, which may present certain obstacles and constraints on collaboration. In some destinations, planning and development may be dictated by undemocratic and politically biased public bodies, in others private vested interests may dominate. In both cases, stakeholder collaboration would be highly desirable but may be hard to bring about.

Progress towards effective joint working may take time. The routes to collaboration may need to reflect traditional structures, with change being introduced gradually, ensuring that initial steps become accepted before others are taken. Rigid models and approaches should be avoided in favour of structures and processes that are flexible and suited to local circumstances.

1.2.2 Creating the Right Processes and Structures for Collaboration

Collaboration can occur simply between two or more stakeholders and could be focused just on one or more selected actions aimed at alleviating poverty. No preconditions need to be met or special structures put in place to enable this to happen.

However, a comprehensive approach to destination management, aimed at poverty alleviation, would be helped by:

- Regular meetings between the key players, who are those best placed to influence the impact of tourism.

- Communication processes with a wider range of stakeholders.

The meeting of key players could occur just once or twice a year, but effective destination management is likely to require quarterly or more frequent meetings.

The key players attending this meeting and working together could be identified loosely as the **destination management (DM) group.** The group could be coordinated through a steering committee. Some initiatives could be pursued through working groups.

A particular function of the DM group could be to oversee the development and implementation of an agreed **tourism strategy** and a joint **plan of action** which addresses poverty alleviation as a primary objective – through following the steps outlined in this manual. The group could also move swiftly to taking action.

Recommendations made in the remainder of this manual are sometimes directed at 'DM groups', meaning no more than the collection of players at the destination level working together on appropriate action.

The DM group could be based on a very loose and informal structure. However, it could also be more formalised as a specifically constituted Destination Management Organisation (DMO). The step to establishing a formal DMO, if this was felt to be appropriate, could be taken at some later stage, after a period of collaborating together on initiatives. DMOs can take many forms[9] but two typical examples are:

- an independent body with a separate constitution and staff, established and run as a joint venture/undertaking by different stakeholder groups; or

- a body or committee established by a local authority and serviced by it, with a membership representing a range of organizations and stakeholder interests.

Whatever structure is adopted, ensuring effective collaboration between different stakeholders requires skill and commitment. Four stages of the collaborative process have been identified:[10]

- **getting started** (bringing the right people together and preparing the ground);

- **determining goals and actions** (discussing expectations; planning and agreeing roles);

- **managing the process** (providing leadership; adopting effective procedures and maintaining commitment);

- **adaptive management** (evaluating results and making improvements).

The **mix** of key players in the DM group may vary from one destination to another. The remainder of this section considers the position of various types of stakeholder (as illustrated on p. 7), their importance in destination management for poverty alleviation and processes of communication with them.

Two very important points to bear in mind are that:

- Some form of DM group or even a DMO may already exist in the destination. The requirement will then be to review its membership, especially with respect to the range of interests represented and the relevance to poverty alleviation.

- **Initiation** and **leadership** of a collaborative process to strengthen destination management and relate it to poverty alleviation could be provided by any type of stakeholder – government agency, local authority, NGO, international agency, private sector network or individual enterprise.

Box 3 Destination management structures in Western Coastal Area, Ghana[11]

In 2006 SNV began working on tourism in western Ghana, in the context of poverty alleviation and the sustainable use of natural resources. They started working separately with a range of different bodies. However, they quickly realised that collaboration among the actors was limited, there was no common vision and very little involvement of private sector tourism enterprises. They therefore changed their strategy in 2008 to a more holistic multi-stakeholder approach within a defined geographical area. They selected the West Coast as a pilot Destination Management Area, covering 4 districts with high poverty levels but clear tourism potential.

SNV was the initiator and catalyst, bringing the stakeholders together. This involved:

- Selling the concept – lobbying and convincing stakeholders.

- Organising and launching a Steering Committee, with ministerial mandate.

- Gaining support from Ghana Tourist Board (GTB) who helped organise the private sector.

- Conducting a Tourism Baseline Study in collaboration with Cape Coast University.

---

9   See World Tourism Organization, 2007.

10   Detailed guidance is provided in World Tourism Organization, 2009.

11   From SNV Ghana.

A key aspect was the organization of the private sector, made up of 20 beach resorts, into a club, who could then participate effectively in the Steering Committee. Other key players include an NGO (Ghana Wildlife Society), a consultancy running a poverty project, Ankasa National Park, the University, GTB, and the Regional Economic Planning Department. Together they have prepared a practical management plan for the destination.

1.2.3 Coordinating the Public Sector

Public sector engagement is critical in the areas of: destination planning and marketing; integrated development between sectors; infrastructure development; standards and regulation; education and training; and data gathering and monitoring on poverty and tourism performance.

The **local authorities** covering the destination should play a central role in its management for the benefit of the local population. They may take the form of a single municipality, group of municipalities or district or provincial level authority, depending on the size of the destination and structure of governance in the country.

It can help if the local authority(ies):

- secures **local political support** for tourism as a tool in poverty alleviation;

- nominates a **lead manager** with overall responsibility for tourism and destination management, who is fully aware of poverty alleviation issues and opportunities. In some cases local authorities may already have a tourism department;

- ensures **engagement and coordination** (possibly through the above manager) with its various departments and functions – notably planning, economic development, environment and education;

- plays a key (potentially **leadership)** role in the DM group, possibly housing its meetings and facilitating joint activity.

National and regional government departments or agencies should be involved, through:

- inviting their direct participation in the DM group, especially where they have a presence in the destination; or

- maintaining regular contact and flow of information with them.

Government departments or agencies of particular relevance to the link between tourism and poverty alleviation include those which:

- have policy or management responsibility for key assets in the destination such as national parks or main cultural sites (e.g. Department of Natural Resources and/or individual park management boards);

- support economic development initiatives in the region in question (e.g. Department of Trade and/ or Regional Development Agency);

- provide support and extension services for small businesses in general and for relevant sectors, such as agriculture or handicrafts, in particular.

1.2.4 Engaging the Private Sector

Private sector tourism enterprises must be involved in the management of the destination as essentially they constitute the tourism sector. Their contribution includes: generating tourist flows, making investments, securing wealth for the area and its population and providing jobs in tourism. They provide the essential link between the destination and tourists and are best placed to understand their needs and interests and influence their activities.

Much of this manual is concerned with understanding the current links between private sector enterprises and poverty (section 1.4), securing private sector response (section 1.7) and taking specific action to channel tourism spending towards the poor through employment, supply chains, philanthropy and other mechanisms (part 2).

Two key types of player are:

- **Tourism service providers.** These include resorts, hotels, restaurants, attractions, activity providers, transport companies, guides, and other kinds of enterprise catering for tourists.

- **Tour operators.** These include:

  - Domestic tour operators, who provide visitor handling, itineraries and programmes in the country. Often they are based in the capital city but some may be located in the destination itself or have representation there. They have a significant influence on tourist behaviour and should be seen as key players wherever they are based.

  - International operators who play a key role in influencing tourist destination choice and are increasingly concerned with supporting communities in the destinations they promote.

Many other types of private sector enterprise are also stakeholders in tourism, such as those providing inputs and services to tourism enterprises through the supply chain. This is described further in section 1.4.

Private sector engagement as partners in the destination management process can be achieved in three ways:

- **Direct involvement of certain individual companies.** Larger scale and knowledgeable service providers and tour operators that are based or active in the destination, or who may be planning investments or programmes there, have a very valuable role to play in securing poverty alleviation using all the mechanisms outlined in part 2. They could be invited to become directly involved in the DM group as well as participating in the various destination management activities. A successful way of influencing the private sector is to work with a few selected enterprises of all sizes on pilot initiatives and use them to influence others in the destination. Some enterprises may already be very engaged in pro-poor tourism initiatives.

- **Direct involvement of representative bodies.** These may include local chambers of trade, more specific bodies such as local tourist associations, or bodies representing specific activities such as hotels associations, guides associations etc. They should be invited to participate directly in the DM group and be encouraged to maintain a link between it and their individual members which may be very small businesses.

- **Consultation with all tourism related enterprises.** All tourism related businesses in the destination should be seen individually as stakeholders. As well as working with whatever representative bodies may exist, ways of consulting and communicating more widely should be found. As well as direct contact, these might include:

  - open meetings and workshops;

  - surveys (an example of an enterprise survey relating to current activity on poverty alleviation is covered in section 1.4).

1.2.5 Benefiting from NGOs, Educational Bodies and Development Assistance Agencies

While relevant to destination management in general, NGOs can play an essential role in all stages of making tourism more pro-poor – from shaping the strategy to direct involvement with actions.

Key contributions that NGOs can make include:

* providing knowledge of poverty issues and priorities in the destination;

* representing the needs of specific groups and poor people in general;

* capacity building, including working with specific projects or with individual communities;

* providing a link to sources of funding.

At the outset it is important to form a picture of which NGOs are active in the country and what they are concerned with. The most relevant NGOs will be those that are actively engaged in the destination, preferably with a local base there. They may be independent local entities or branches of national or international NGOs. Particularly useful NGOs include those whose objectives relate to:

* poverty alleviation, including local economic development and business development (which may or may not already include tourism);

* representation and empowerment of indigenous communities and their culture;

* employees rights – such as trade (labour) unions;

* natural resource management and sustainable livelihoods;

* representation and empowerment of women and minority groups;

* verification and certification of pro-poor tourism and sustainability claims.

Key NGOs should be invited to participate in the DM group. Others may be consulted and kept informed on a regular basis, but with the option to engage them more fully as and when needed to provide particular advice or to help deliver specific initiatives.

Bodies concerned with education and training, especially at a technical level, can make a valuable input, providing advice and expertise to the DM group and assisting directly with research and capacity building.

Development assistance agencies, including international technical assistance and funding agencies active in the country, can also play an important role in making tourism more pro-poor, through influencing policy, providing knowledge, strengthening local institutions and delivering funding. They can act as important catalysts for multi-stakeholder working in destinations at the early stages, but it is important that collaborative structures do not come to rely on them in the longer term.

1.2.6 Engaging Local Residents

Local residents in the destination are stakeholders in tourism, through the positive or negative impact it may have on them. The destination management process must engage them, especially those who may be targeted through pro-poor actions. Their interests may be represented by the local authority and especially by local NGOs, but this is unlikely to be sufficient.

Local residents should be considered both as individuals and as members of community groupings. The latter may be defined geographically (e.g. individual towns, neighbourhoods, or villages) socio-culturally (e.g. indigenous and ethnic groupings; women; young people) or by interest or activity (e.g. employees working in the hospitality sector or in the supply chain). Working with local community groups or developing community representative organizations can greatly improve the effectiveness of working with local communities.

Engagement may take a number of forms:

- general awareness-raising across the destination, for example through seeking coverage in local media, open meetings etc.;

- inviting participation from community representatives in the DM group or in specific working groups;

- work with residents and community groups by individual stakeholders (e.g. private sector enterprises engaging directly with neighbouring communities);

- specific engagement programmes with identified communities, working with them to plan, develop or strengthen tourism activities (see section 1.7).

Two-way interaction with residents through the processes listed above should seek to provide a better understanding of: current involvement in tourism; skills gaps; other barriers to participation; cultural/social issues relating to tourism; and overall aspirations.

1.2.7 Communicating with Tourists

Finally, tourists in the destination are also stakeholders in its management. How they respond is a critical factor in delivering benefit and alleviating poverty.

It is virtually impossible to engage tourists directly in destination management. However, other ways should be found of establishing a two way communication with tourists – obtaining input (views, interests) from them and providing them with information. Four mechanisms include:

- carrying out visitor surveys;

- using direct communication material, such as destination websites and print;

- working through tour operators and service providers, who can engage directly with tourists and should be actively encouraged to provide feedback from them to the DM group;

- working with international and domestic media, such as travel journalists and producers of guidebooks, who are hugely influential in communicating key aspects of the destination to tourists, and are increasingly covering issues relating to tourism impact and effects on poverty.

Communication with tourists in the ways listed above should show them how their behaviour can more or less benefit the poor – for example in their patterns of spending, including purchase of local products and services, and engagement in the various activities described in part 2 of this manual.

1.2 Listing the main payers and considering how they communicate

1 The destination in which you are interested may already be quite actively engaged in destination management and may have some form of structure or processes for engaging different stakeholders in this. Note down what you know about what is happening: Who is involved? How are they coordinated? What are the bottlenecks to collaboration?

2 Think about the local authorities in the destination and the higher level public sector bodies involved in activities affecting tourism and poverty alleviation.

  – Which local authority(ies) are best placed to influence tourism development and local response to this? Are they actively engaged?

  – Are there particular national or regional government departments or agencies that should be more actively involved?

3 Think about the private sector enterprises involved in tourism.

   – Do you know which tour operators are most active in bringing tourists to the destination?

   – What are the main enterprises providing tourism services?

   – Are there any bodies linking and representing the different tourism enterprises, large and small?

   – How good are the communication mechanisms with all the above?

4 Consider and list the NGOs and agencies supporting poverty alleviation in and around the destination – promoting development, managing resources, empowering minorities, providing education, providing funding.

   – Which ones do you feel are best placed to get involved in pro-poor tourism development and provide knowledge, advice and support?

5 What type of coordination mechanism do you feel is most suitable for bringing the main players together, given the circumstances in the destination?

6 Are there existing ways of communicating directly with local community groups about tourism? How might they be strengthened?

7 What mechanisms currently exist for communicating with tourists coming to the destination? How might they be strengthened?

1.3 Identifying Who Should Benefit and Their Needs

At the outset, it will be important for everyone involved to agree a shared view of who should be seen as the poor in the particular context of the destination in question. Who in particular should and can benefit through tourism and in what ways? Without this, an assessment cannot be made of the extent to which tourism is currently pro-poor and how and where it should be developed or changed to make it more so. It would also not be possible in future to know the contribution that tourism has made to alleviating poverty, or the impact of specific initiatives.

Working at a destination level has advantages in this respect. It enables priorities for poverty alleviation to be considered across quite a wide area, but also to be close enough to the ground to understand local circumstances and needs.

1.3.1 Forming a Broad View of Poverty in the Destination

Poverty has many dimensions and there are many definitions of who should be regarded as the poor. Globally, poverty is assessed by the standards of the poorest countries but in discussing poverty in individual countries it is important to recognise that different measures may be relevant to different circumstances. Also, national indicators often hide important differences between regions.

A common method used to measure poverty is based on incomes or consumption levels. A basic indicator of the level of poverty in an area is the headcount index, which is the proportion of people living in households below a previously determined national poverty line. The **poverty line** is the minimum level of income deemed necessary to meet basic needs in a given country. At a global level, extreme poverty is considered to exist below a general poverty line of US$ 1.25 a day at 2005 prices.[12]

---

12   By this measure, 1.4 billion people in the world are poor (Ravallion and Chen, 2008).

However poverty lines vary, as what is necessary to satisfy basic needs will vary across time and place. Availability at a sub-national level of recent data, usually gathered through household surveys, will vary between countries. If reasonably accurate data is available locally, comparisons can be made between different locations within one destination. Other basic monetary measures include personal income or GDP[13] per capita.

The headcount index tells us nothing about the distribution of consumption or income. The level of inequality may also be important and can be measured in different ways. It has been found that the higher the initial inequality in a country, the less the gains from growth are shared by the poor.[14]

Poverty is not just an economic condition however. Social and environmental issues play their part in human wellbeing. For some, alleviating poverty is as much about **providing opportunity** as about providing income. Access to health care, education, and basic resources and infrastructure may be used to determine who is poor. Statistics such as levels of enrolment in education, adult literacy, access to clean water, child mortality and life expectancy can be used, amongst others, as measures of these aspects of poverty. Non-monetary data of this type is becoming increasingly easy to obtain.

Small area estimates are often available plotted on maps[15] showing the spatial distribution of different dimensions of poverty, which can present complex information in a visual format that is easy to understand.

All the above data can be used to:

- obtain an overall picture of the level and type of poverty in a destination;

- identify areas within the destination with the greatest levels of poverty.

However, rather than simply relying on basic statistics, contact should be maintained with relevant government agencies and NGOs working on poverty alleviation in the area. They can provide more information and ideas on:

- local poverty – its level, location and nature; and

- how tourism can complement economic activity in other sectors and other pro-poor initiatives.

1.3.2 Identifying Target Beneficiaries

Having understood the basic dimensions of poverty, more thought should be given to the kinds of people to target and how they might be identified.

At its very simplest, tourism will be pro-poor if it is able to provide income earning opportunities for local people who are below or close to the national poverty line, in or reasonably close to their home environment. There is a strong likelihood that, at the outset, such people will be unskilled or semi-skilled.

In some circumstances, this simple approach – focussing on local unskilled or semi-skilled people – may be sufficient to guide policy and action. However, consideration may also be given to other factors, such as levels and types of inequality as mentioned above. Selecting an appropriate approach may require careful thought. Some questions to think about when considering target beneficiaries include:

- **The breadth as against the depth of impact.** Is it more important to make a marginal difference to a lot of people or a great difference to a few?

---

13 The total value of all goods and services produced in an area, including government and private sector investment, personal consumption etc.

14 Looking at global figures, many who escape absolute poverty by the US$ 1.25 per day standard are still poor by the median poverty line of US$ 2 a day; in fact the number of people living between US$ 1.25 and US$ 2 a day doubled between 1981 and 2005.

15 Useful information on the use of poverty maps in policy making is available in World Bank, 2007.

- **The effect on the poorest or most marginalised.** Should tourism somehow provide benefit for those most in need in society, including especially poor communities or families and individuals who cannot access education or who have particular disabilities or health problems? Whereas it may not be practicable for them to become directly engaged in tourism, they can benefit from indirect linkages between tourism and other activities and from investment in social infrastructure supported by tourism. Furthermore, this group should certainly be protected against negative impacts of tourism.

- **Gender issues.** What priority should be given to women as beneficiaries? In some societies, women may be more vulnerable and suffer more than men from poverty of opportunity as well as low levels of income. It has been shown that women are more likely than men to ensure that any increase in income benefits the whole family group.

- **The needs of young people.** Giving young people a better start in life and providing them with training and career opportunities can be very important in strengthening the future chances of communities coming out of poverty.

- **Location.** Considering regional disparities, which parts of the destination are most in need? Consideration should be given to the relative levels of poverty in rural as against urban areas and in the remoter or more accessible communities.

In thinking about these questions of different target beneficiaries, it will be important to balance the choice of those who might benefit with consideration of who it might be possible and most practicable to reach through tourism.

1.3.3 Understanding Needs and Barriers

Having identified the level and nature of poverty in the destination and the sections of the poor to target, it is essential to seek to understand more about their needs. This may require additional research and investigation, including possible surveys of households (see example in box 4).

An important issue is the structure of the existing economy and current sources of livelihood in poor communities. Key questions to consider are:

- **Levels of economic need.** Some individuals and communities may only require relatively small levels of additional income to make a difference, which may be achieved, for example, through a small uplift in sales.

- **Livelihood patterns.** It will be important to consider the relative need for full time or part-time jobs. Often, tourism income can be a valuable supplement to income from other activities and provide one component of multiple occupations. This may fit well with the nature of tourism employment. On the other hand, competing demands from tourism for people's time can interrupt traditional work patterns (this is covered more fully in Annex 1 – see below).

- **Environmental and social issues.** Livelihood and wellbeing in communities are affected by impacts of tourism which are not directly economic. Consideration should be given to the vulnerability of different communities in the destination to possible negative impacts of tourism development on their environment, access to resources such as water and land, cultural integrity and social structures. This should be balanced against possible positive impacts from improvements to infrastructure, skills and other assets. Again, see Annex 1 for more detail.

At the same time, consideration should be given to the barriers facing target beneficiaries, which affect their ability to respond to tourism opportunities. These may include: social structures; basic educational levels; image and awareness issues; health and accessibility.

The above considerations should play an important part in determining the strategies and actions which are taken in a destination to develop pro-poor tourism. This is covered further in section 1.6 below and in part 2.

Annex 1 contains a consideration of tourism impacts on poor communities based on the 'Livelihoods Approach' – an analysis model that takes a comprehensive approach to issues affecting the poor and includes links to tools that help with the analysis.

Box 4 Shaping a project around an understanding of poverty, Bhutan[16]

The 9th and 10th Five Year Plan for tourism in Bhutan included the objectives of spreading the economic benefits of tourism more widely in the country, involving local communities in tourism and diversifying the product offer. In selecting action to fulfil this, the Tourism Council of Bhutan (TCB) and the Department of Forestry in consultation with the private sector considered various parts of the country. A group of communities in the central south were chosen for a pilot project, owing to the diversified appeal of the landscape, the potential to create a new walking trail there, the reasonable accessibility and the economic fragility of the area which was highly dependent on agriculture. The Association of Bhutanese Tour Operators (and its members) was involved from the beginning in order to check out the relevance of the project for the market and to provide market access.

Before fixing on the project, however, a very thorough analysis was undertaken of the level and nature of poverty in the area, the needs of the community and their reaction to tourism. Existing data sources were used initially, including the Household Census of the National Statistics Bureau and a previous local socio-economic study. However, to gain a more detailed picture of need and how this might be addressed by tourism the TCB conducted its own household baseline survey using interviews covering income, occupation, gender issues, lifestyle, basic needs and attitudes to tourism. The results revealed that 23% of households surveyed had no cash income at all and half had inadequate food supply in some months. All those interviewed were interested in tourism as an opportunity to supplement cash income.

The project proceeded to establish the Nabji-Korphu trail – a guided trekking route. Data collected after one year of operation showed that a small number of visits (6 groups totalling 70 tourists in 2007) could make a valuable difference. In the first year US$ 4,000 was earned in total by the communities with almost 72% of the households taking a share of this through portering, cooking, selling vegetables and handicraft. Most people surveyed subsequently felt they had benefited economically, spending the cash on food, clothing, education, seeds and in other ways. Socio-cultural and environmental impact was also assessed and found to be broadly positive.

Without the initial analysis of poverty and need, it would not have been possible to shape the project correctly or to have a basis upon which to judge success not in terms of total income but in terms of relative alleviation of poverty.

The TCB used the results of the Nabji-Korphu trek project to inform the development of more business-orientated approaches to community-managed tourism products.

 **1.3 Considering sources of knowledge on poverty**

1 Think about the likely sources of statistics on poverty in the destination – do you think they are reasonably reliable and will give information for different parts of the destination?

2 Identify the NGOs best placed to tell you about the poverty situation and needs in the destination.

3 Consider possible target beneficiaries – types of people and locations.

4 What do you know about the target beneficiaries – their needs and vulnerabilities? How might you gain more information and analyse the situation?

---

16   From SNV Bhutan with data referenced Dorji, 2007.

1.4 Understanding How Tourism Is Working Currently and Who Is Benefiting

In order to strengthen the performance of tourism and deliver more benefits to the poor, it is necessary to have a clear understanding of how tourism is functioning in the destination and who is currently benefiting. This requires some systematic analysis, which should be instigated by the DM group, with the support of all the stakeholders discussed in section 1.2.

This section sets out the different stages of a suggested analysis process. Much of the information gathering outlined here is normally needed to guide the preparation of any tourism strategy for a destination, which requires an understanding of visitor volumes and trends, visitor spending, the number and type of tourism enterprises and their performance, knowledge of current markets and visitor satisfaction. However, the process outlined here places an additional emphasis on looking at the recipients of tourism income and their circumstances, in order to guide policy and action on making tourism more pro-poor.

In some destinations much of this information may already be available, in others almost all of it may need to be gathered for the first time. It is important, however, that the data gathering and analysis should not be too onerous and hold up progress towards taking action. This is really all about asking some straightforward questions of different stakeholders and considering their answers.

1.4.1 Identifying the Tourism Value Chain for a Destination

Before looking in detail at the stages of data gathering and analysis referred to above, it is helpful to consider a conceptual model, the tourism value chain, that provides the basis for the analysis.

Tourism at the level of the destination is a complex economic sector, because the product that is produced and consumed is the overall **visitor experience.** This can be described as a linked set of components (with associated influences, consumption patterns and expenditure) over space and time, which include:

- pre departure images, information and booking;

- journey to the destination, arrival and orientation;

- use of accommodation and catering facilities;

- purchases of personal items and souvenirs;

- visits to attractions and participation in activities;

- departure and journey home (or to another destination);

- memories and post visit contact.

Each of these components, which involves **transactions** and expenditure by the tourist, are provided and delivered by a large number of different players in both the public and private sectors. They include travel agents, tour operators, transport providers, hotels, restaurants, attraction site managers, activity operators, handicraft sellers, general retailers, and others. Many will be located in the destination itself but some will not be.

Each of the enterprises or organizations above will in turn need to enter into a further set of transactions with other enterprises or organizations (both within and outside the destination) in order to create their particular component of the visitor experience. For example, restaurants need to purchase food from farmers (or from wholesalers, who in turn purchase from farmers).

The comprehensive set of components which make up the visitor's experience, together with all the transactions associated with them, is sometimes called the tourism value chain (TVC). A schematic illustration of a TVC is shown in figure 3.

Figure 3   A tourism value chain for a destination visit

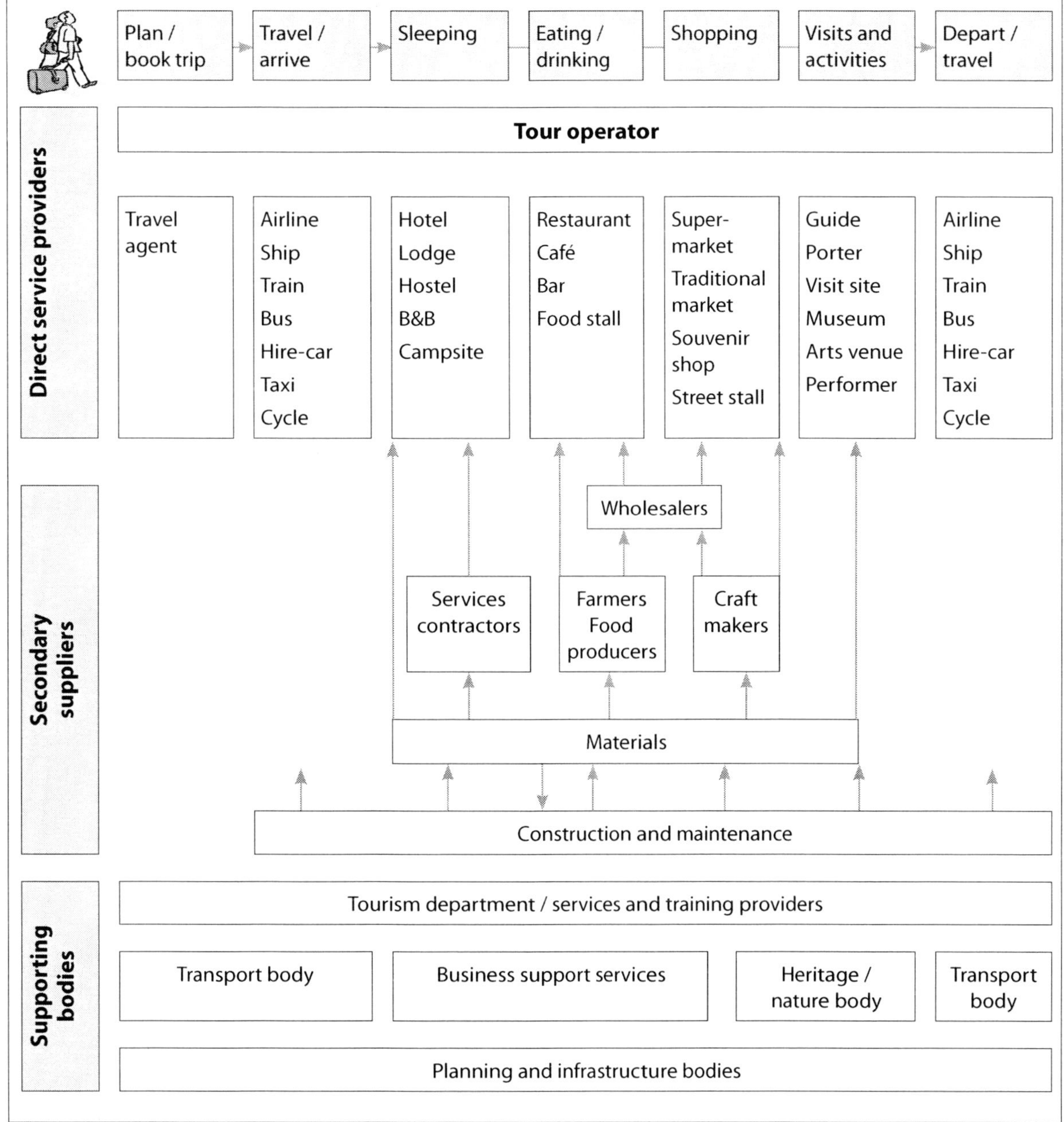

The sum total of all the transactions will constitute the economic value generated by the visitor experience. Value Chain Analysis (VCA) is a term used for the process of investigating the structure and working of a value chain and the economic value generated.

Destinations concerned about poverty alleviation will be interested in:

- The total amount of income from all these transactions that is received in the destination and, within this, the amount that is received by the poor.

- The particular kinds of transaction which are most pro-poor in terms of:

    - the total amount of income from them that reaches the poor;

    - the proportion of income from them that reaches the poor.[17]

---

17   At the same time, they should be aware that it may be necessary for some transactions to undertaken by, or to benefit, people outside the destination or the non-poor, in order for the local poor to benefit at all.

VCA does not necessarily involve an analysis of benefit received by the poor, but it often does so; such analysis is sometimes referred to as PPI (pro-poor impact) analysis. SNV has undertaken or supported many studies[18] involving analysis of the tourism value chain and its pro-poor impact.

1.4.2 Analysing the Tourism Value Chain and its Pro-poor Impact

The main purpose of the analysis should be:

*   to form an overall picture of tourism in the area;

*   to understand income flows and the level of participation by the poor;

*   to provide baseline information against which future changes and impacts can be measured.

However, during the gathering of information to fulfil these purposes it is sensible to take the opportunity also to probe wider issues, such as market trends and stakeholders' perceptions of barriers and future opportunities.

Table 1 outlines the steps to take.

NB: Detailed and specific guidance on each of these steps is provided in Annex 2. This is an essential part of this manual and all readers should consult this annex.

When combined with the information about the tourism potential of the area, which will be covered in section 1.5, such an analysis of the tourism value chain will enable strategic directions and actions to be determined, as will be discussed in section 1.6.

Table 1   Steps in tourism value chain and pro-poor impact analysis

Step		Purpose	Action
1	**Conduct initial stakeholder interviews and consultation**	To get an overview of tourism in the area, how it functions and what the challenges are in delivering more benefit to the poor.	• Initiate discussions in the DM group. • Interview the public bodies, main tour operators, representative organizations and NGOs. • Hold a workshop with invited stakeholders.
2	**Create an inventory of tourism facilities and services**	To provide initial quantification of the size and shape of the sector and baseline data with which to work.	• Assemble information on all types of tourism services and related enterprises. • Use a wide variety of sources, including written records and personal local knowledge. • Record basic information including ownership, location, size etc.
3	**Assemble market and performance knowledge**	To strengthen understanding of context and trends using any available information that may exist.	• Investigate all published data on tourism in the destination or relevant data at a regional or national level. • Record any performance knowledge gained from Step 1.
4	**Identify types of job/activity most relevant to the target poor**	To provide a basis for knowing and measuring what is pro-poor and what is not.	• Consider who are the poor in the destination. • Specify what to look out for that would benefit them – e.g. jobs accessible to unskilled people.

18   Much of the pioneering work in this field, which has informed this manual, has been undertaken by the Overseas Development Institute (ODI) (www.odi.org.uk) (1-11-2009).

Step		Purpose	Action
5	**Identify sub-chains and categorise enterprises/ service**	To enable results to be related to types of tourism and to focus the analysis on aspects of greatest interest.	• Place enterprises into identifiable categories/ clusters. • Consider whether and how to prioritise the research/analysis.
6	**Conduct enterprise survey/ interviews**	To measure economic performance, the extent to which employment and spending by enterprises is pro-poor, and the factors which affect this.	• Draw up a representative sample of enterprises to survey. • Inform/engage the enterprises. • Prepare a questionnaire to use. • Conduct the survey.
7	**Conduct visitor survey**	To check spending patterns by different types of tourist, capture data on incidental purchases not reflected by enterprises, and gain insight into factors influencing spending decisions.	• Prepare a questionnaire relevant to the destination. • Identify survey sites where visitors can be intercepted at the end of their stay. • Conduct the survey.
8	**Aggregate results**	To provide quantified estimates which indicate what proportion of what types of tourism is pro-poor.	• Undertake systematic calculations that combine the results from the various steps. • Relate the results to the categories of enterprise and sub-chains identified.
9	**Draw conclusions**	To use the findings to point to priority opportunities, strategies and actions to most effectively reach the poor.	• Reflect on the meaning and implications of the above calculations. • Draw on the qualitative insights and feedback gained from all the steps.

1.4.3 Shaping Value Chain Analysis to Match Available Resources

A full value chain analysis as set out in table 1 and elaborated in more detail in Annex 2 can be a time consuming process. However it can be approached in various ways to suit the resources available for carrying it out.

The research and analysis could be carried out internally over time by a small team of people selected by the DM group. However, consideration should be given to either or both of the following:

- **A participatory approach.** Here, a deliberate policy of involving different stakeholders in gathering information is adopted. One reason is to save time; another is to raise awareness of the issues and interest in the results.

- **Use of external technical assistance.** Destinations may benefit from bringing in people with experience of the process, in order to maximise efficiency, avoid pitfalls, make use of knowledge from other areas, and add value to the analysis.

It may not be possible to achieve a fully comprehensive picture based on accurate data. This will partly depend on the size of the destination and the time and budget available. However, a broad picture and very approximate results may be all that is required.

In some destinations, intense and rapid exercises have been carried out, lasting no more than two weeks, which have been able to draw very helpful conclusions to guide policy. An example is given in box 5. This kind of approach is greatly helped by careful preparatory work beforehand to assemble initially available information and prepare the stakeholders for the exercise.

Box 5 Tracing the Tourism Dollar in Northern Tanzania[19]

Tourism in Tanzania is largely concentrated in the north of the country. Working with SNV, the Overseas Development Institute (ODI) analysed the impact on the poor of the tourism value chains associated with two particularly important tourist products - mountain climbing on Kilimanjaro and safari game viewing. They used a rapid appraisal technique, developed by ODI, involving intensive work by a small team over a two week period. This involved:

- Using structured questionnaires to interview tourism service providers, including tour operators, based at key geographic locations; a representative sample was drawn up using SNV's prior knowledge.

- A survey of tourists departing from Kilimanjaro International Airport, having completed their holiday.

The information gathered was synthesised to produce a pro-poor analysis of the value chains for each of the two tourist products, and an estimate was made of the pro-poor impact of each component of tourist expenditure. To illustrate the approach, the table below has been constructed from the results for the Kilimanjaro trek (the results from the safari circuit are not illustrated here but the approach is similar).

The study found that 28% of the tourist expenditure from climbing Kilimanjaro reached the poor. The equivalent for the safari circuit was less at 19%. However, far greater numbers participate in the latter (300,000 as compared with 35,000), meaning that the safari circuit has a much larger impact on poverty alleviation overall.

Detailed analysis of the impact of spending enabled the study to draw some specific conclusions of relevance to policy. The greatest benefit to the poor from climbing Kilimanjaro came from wages and tips to the guides, porters and cooks required to support the trek, which comprised only 18% of the total visitor spend but provided 62% of the tourism value which reached the poor.

The analysis can also be used to point out the benefits to the poor which might result from a marginal increase in certain activities. For example, it was found that craft and souvenir selling on the safari circuit was generating a livelihood for around 28,000 workers and that any increase in spending on crafts would have a significant pro-poor impact.

---

19   Mitchell et al., 2009.

Value chain analysis for Kilimanjaro trek

In-country spend per tourist = cost of package (US$ 1,205) + discretionary spend (US$ 171) = US$ 1,376

Component	Tour operator	Transport	Accommodation	Food and beverage	Cultural goods and services	Wages and tips	Park fees	Total visit
Spend per component	US$ 223	US$ 40	US$ 84	US$ 80	US$ 58	US$ 242	US$ 649	US$ 1,376
Component as % of spend per visit	16%	3%	6%	6%	4%	18%	47%	100%
% of component spend considered pro-poor	0%	0%	16%	90%	50%	100%	5%	-
Pro-poor expenditure per component	-	-	US$ 13	US$ 72	US$ 29	US$ 242	US$ 32	US$ 389
% of total pro-poor expenditure	0%	0%	3%	19%	7%	62%	8%	100%
% of spend per visit which is considered pro-poor								28%
Total annual pro-poor impact of Kilimanjaro trek product:								
Number of visits made or packages sold annually								35,000
Total annual in-country expenditure								US$ 50 million
Total annual pro-poor expenditure								US$ 13 million
% of total annual in-country expenditure which is considered pro-poor								28%

It is important to emphasise that while a comprehensive value chain analysis may be desirable this may well not be practicable for the destination, yet a simplified or partial version can still provide helpful guidance. By taking a relatively quick look at the how tourism is operating in the area and the flow of income to the poor, it would then be possible to select some particular parts of the value chain (e.g. some specific sectors or products) which appear to offer potential and to focus more detailed consultation and analysis around them. An illustration of this approach is provided in box 6.

Box 6 Focussing interventions in Luang Prabang, Laos[20]

In 2006 a study was undertaken by an external consultant to assist the provincial tourism administration of Luang Prabang to understand how poor people were participating in the tourism economy and what opportunities existed to increase their participation and earnings in different parts of the tourism value chain. A very quick analysis was undertaken, sufficient to paint the big picture and point to areas for more detailed investigation leading to intervention. A rough and ready mapping of overall financial flows was carried out. Based on this, an assessment of income flowing to the poor was undertaken for the main sectors of tourist expenditure: accommodation; food and drink; handicrafts; and rural excursions.

The study used established tourism data on supply (amount and size of different enterprises) and demand (market data) and a set of interviews with tourism businesses, direct suppliers of goods and services (employees, sellers) and consumers. Only a very small number of interviews were conducted in each case. It was felt that they did provide a sufficiently representative set of results, but caveats on the reliability of the figures were issued.

The results suggested that although accommodation accounted for the highest turnover amongst the four sectors only around 6% of this reached the poor (taken as semi skilled or unskilled people) partly owing to low wage rates. In contrast they received around 40-50% of turnover in the food and handicrafts sectors and 33% in transport and excursions. The knowledge gained from the interviews pointed to specific opportunities for pro-poor interventions in the latter sectors, namely: increasing supplies of fresh food; strengthening supplies of silk, silver and wood for handicrafts; and increasing spending on rural excursions through increasing the proportion of tourists staying overnight and their opportunities to buy directly from villagers.

These opportunities were taken up by SNV. A more detailed study of villager engagement in rural excursions was undertaken, involving interviewing and mapping the actors, beneficiaries and flow of services and money for four different excursions. Tour operators were interviewed to gauge market trends and various constraints and opportunities were identified. This led to a decision to focus on adding value to existing attractions and improving their pro-poor orientation, rather than developing new excursions. A market driven strategy was adopted, focussed on expanding and improving micro-enterprises.

1.4 Thinking about data on the operation and impact of tourism

1 The amount of data and information available on the current structure and performance of tourism will vary between destinations. In your destination:

   – How well do you believe that the tourism value chain is understood (look again at figure 3)?

   – For each step of the analysis outlined in table 1 and Annex 2, think about what information may be already available.

2 Consider how gaps in knowledge can best be filled. Think about how you would go about:

   – Creating the inventory of facilities (step 2) and assembling information on markets and performance (step 3).

   – Conducting a survey of enterprises (step 6).

   – Conducting a visitor survey (step 7).

3 For the above activity, how could you engage the interest of different stakeholders? Would you need external technical assistance?

4 Think about the different sectors and types of tourism in your destination. At this stage, before doing an analysis, which ones do you guess are likely to generate most income for the poor:

   – In absolute terms – i.e. the total amount reaching the poor?

   – In relative terms – i.e. the proportion of the income from the sector that reaches the poor?

1.5 Judging the Destination's Future Potential for Tourism that Benefits the Poor

A clear understanding of the destination's current tourism performance and impact, as outlined in the previous section, provides one set of evidence for the destination management plan and pro-poor action. However, it is also necessary to consider a range of external and internal factors that will affect the destination's future tourism potential and opportunities for poverty alleviation. These factors, considered in this section, include market potential, availability of tourism assets, resource limitations and constraints and the destination's position with respect to other destinations.

Consideration of these factors is essential in all destination planning. However, once again, we have looked at them especially from a pro-poor perspective.

1.5.1 Balancing Market and Product Development

An objective of any strategy aimed at poverty alleviation through tourism should be to generate more income for the destination and for the poor within it through increasing the amount and type of spending by new or existing visitors. This requires careful consideration of whether to focus on strengthening products or on reaching new markets, which can be helped using a simple matrix as in table 2.

Table 2   Product-Market Matrix[21]

<table>
<tr><td rowspan="2">Market</td><td></td><td colspan="2">Product</td></tr>
<tr><td></td><td>EXISTING</td><td>NEW</td></tr>
<tr><td rowspan="1">EXISTING</td><td colspan="1"></td><td>1 Market penetration

= Selling more of an existing product to an existing market.

Low risk strategy but will supply outstrip demand and lead to price drop and lack of viability?</td><td>2 Product development

= Selling a new or improved product to an existing market.

Can stimulate more spending by existing visitors and increase total income to poor communities, but products need to match market interests.</td></tr>
<tr><td>NEW</td><td></td><td>3 Market development

= Selling an existing product to a new market.

Can be hard for poor communities to do on their own, but a destination should consider whether there are new markets that it can realistically attract and from which the poor can then benefit.</td><td>4 Diversification

= Selling a new product to a new market.

Hard and high risk for poor communities. Would require participation of an established enterprise with a large marketing budget backed by the destination.</td></tr>
</table>

A common option is to continue with established products and seek to sell more of them to existing markets (1). This requires little new innovation and investment and as such is appropriate for poor producers who should avoid risk. However, penetration of the market may already be high with little opportunity for more sales of the same product. Many people trying to sell the same product or service to the same visitors, as is often the case in poor communities, can lead to inefficiency, cut-throat competition, depressed prices and low levels of income for the poor.

Developing new products and services for existing markets (2) can be a sensible strategy, strengthening the appeal of the destination as a whole, leading to longer stays, increasing the amount of spend

---

21   Based on Ansoff's Matrix, a classic tool in marketing panning, and adapted from Goodwin, 2006.

per visit and helping it to reach more people. This requires a good understanding of existing visitors' interests, the time they have available, and gaps in existing provision, perhaps helped by some market research and product testing.

In many cases product development does not have to entail establishing an entirely new product. Much can often be achieved by improving an existing product, in terms of quality, style, level of service and possibly price. Again, sound market feedback is essential to guide what improvements to make.

There may well be opportunities to reach new markets. This is a matter to be addressed at a destination level. Market expansion could occur partly by getting more of the same kinds of visitor to come – in a sense, this is a form of increased market penetration (1) as far as the destination is concerned. It could also occur through attracting new kinds of visitor – market development (3) – focussing on those to whom the destination's assets may appeal. Relevance and opportunities for the poor should be borne in mind in any consideration of new target markets.

1.5.2 Understanding Current and Potential Markets

The above considerations underline the importance of undertaking some market research in order to understand as much as possible about existing visitors to the destination and potential new visitor markets. Too often, individual initiatives or projects specifically aimed at generating income for poor communities through tourism have failed because they have not been based on sufficient market knowledge.

The purpose of understanding markets is to:

- Select particular market segments (types of visitor) to prioritise in future, based on considering the ones which:

  - might contribute most to the destination's objectives, including poverty alleviation which depends partly on the amount of spending in the destination;

  - are most likely to be attracted to the destination and to individual products and experiences that are, or could be, offered there, including those that involve the poor;

  - can be accessed and communicated with practicably and cost effectively.

- Identify products to improve or develop and marketing techniques to use that are relevant to those market segments.

Therefore, in investigating different market segments, evidence should be obtained about their:

- Size and growth – numbers in the destination and country, size of the source market, and whether increasing.

- Travel patterns – types of area visited, flexibility and likely length of stay in a destination.

- Spending – whether they are high or low spenders per day, what they spend their money on, and their likely willingness to support poor communities.

- Motivations and needs – the kinds of experience that they are looking for.

- Use of information sources – the media and other material that they use to select a destination and plan their activities.

Four priorities are to:

- **Thoroughly understand existing visitors to the destination.** Their importance has been confirmed above. Recent visitors to the destination provide the best clues about likely future visitors and may themselves be, or become, repeat visitors. They may include a number of different market segments (including those listed in the bullet point below) and it will be important to find out about each of them in considering which ones to prioritise.

- **Investigate domestic and international travel patterns within the country as a whole.** It can be far easier for individual destinations to reach people living in or already visiting elsewhere in the country, perhaps making regular return trips. They may respond well to the kinds of products and experiences that involve the poor. Consider:

  - Tour operators – their current itineraries and the products they promote. Communication with them is usually relatively straightforward.

  - Independent international travellers, who can be more flexible in their travel patterns and purchasing than tour groups.

  - Domestic markets, including expatriates and more affluent urban dwellers. Often they can generate more stable, year round business than international tourists. Domestic markets have seen recent rapid growth in a number of developing countries.

  - Business travellers and visitors to friends/family – they may have particular reasons to come to the destination and may show potential for add-on trips, activities and spending.

- **Consider niche market opportunities.** Some market segments can be identified by special interests that dictate their travel choices and activities – such as wildlife watching, ethnic music or hiking. These may be particularly relevant to the destination's assets. They may also present valuable opportunities for engaging the poor.

- **Reflect national and international trends.** Certain underlying market trends may affect future levels and types of tourism in the destination and the potential response to different types of product. The following have a particular bearing on pro-poor tourism:

  - Growing numbers of tourists seeking authentic, meaningful experiences and interface with local people, as well as more adventurous travel.

  - Increasing proportions of tourists saying that they are concerned about the impact of their travel on host populations.

  - Growing awareness amongst tour operators of these issues, reflected in their selection of products and their communication with customers and suppliers.

  - Recent coverage of poverty issues in international guidebooks, together with advice to readers on activities and opportunities that benefit local communities.

  - Huge advances in cost-effective communication possibilities with independent travellers through the internet.

Market understanding can be achieved through a variety of activities. Some of these were included in the process of investigating current tourism in the destination alongside gathering information for value chain analysis, as set out in section 1.4. and Annex 2.

Actions to pursue include:

- looking at any published tourism statistics for the destination and country;

- conducting a visitor survey in the destination;

- perusing tour operator brochures for the country;

- holding discussions with tour operators, selected tourism enterprises, and especially with guides operating in the destination and elsewhere in the country;

- obtaining and reading guidebooks used by tourists;

- obtaining feedback from trade, media and visitors at any travel shows attended;

- looking at the experience of comparable destinations elsewhere (see later);

- using UNWTO data sources on international tourism trends.

1.5.3 Prioritising Markets and Selecting Approaches to Them

A greater understanding of existing and potential markets will help in making strategic choices about which ones to prioritise and how to gain more benefit from them. As illustrated in the Ansoff Matrix in section 1.5.1 above, the approach may be to:

- gain more spending and pro-poor benefit from existing markets (from the same visitors or more of them), through further promoting and improving existing products and through developing new products; or

- seek to attract some new markets which may already show strong signs of potential in the county and relate well to the destination's assets.

Many destinations find the first approach the easiest to achieve.

Important factors to bear in mind when prioritising markets and thinking about the products and services to improve or to develop include:

- **The number and frequency of visits.**

  Markets accounting for large numbers of visitors may have a greater net effect on poverty in the destination than smaller markets. In considering volume it is necessary to look at both the number of visitors and the frequency of visits per year.

- **The length of stay in the destination.**

  The longer people stay in a destination the greater will be their local economic impact. People on special interest visits, such as birdwatchers sometimes stay longer. Some backpackers may pass through a destination quite quickly, but can be more flexible than other markets and be tempted to stay longer. Getting people to stay overnight rather than just visiting on a day trip makes a big difference, with implications for improving the quality of local accommodation and the availability of activities that fill their time (including evening and early morning experiences).

- **The amount of spending per day.**

  The amount of spending in the destination will affect the impact on the local economy. Some types of tourist will spend much more than others. Up-market segments - people taking more expensive trips and staying in higher price accommodation – may spend more per day in the destination than travellers on a low budget. Simply improving the actual opportunities to spend money locally can help, addressing the availability and quality of local goods and services and their suitability to the markets in question.

- **The nature of their spending.**

  Some types of spending will be more likely than others to benefit the poor. For example, a low proportion of the spending by up-market tourists or those on inclusive tours may be on purchases made directly from the poor, but their spending may reach the poor by virtue of their employment in larger accommodation or catering enterprises or through their participation in the supply chains of these enterprises. Independent travellers, on the other hand, may make more purchases directly from the poor.

The above comments about market behaviour should be taken only as a guide. Visitor behaviour will vary according to the particular circumstances of each destination. This shows the importance of reviewing in detail the available evidence, based on analysis of the value chain as set out in 1.4.

Box 7 Cambodia market comparisons[22]

A Mekong Private Sector Development Facility (MPDF) study in Cambodia in 2008 collected data on expenditure from a range of different market segments and, through analysing the activities and products on which spending was made, was able to compare relative impact on the poor. The analysis looked separately at group and independent travellers from various regional and western countries.

The results suggested that to draw clear conclusions about which segments are most pro-poor requires detailed consideration of visit and spending patterns.

The segments that generate most income for the poor per trip were not necessarily the same as those that generated most per day. Highest levels of pro-poor employment income (PPEI) per person (i.e. per trip) were from Japanese, Chinese and American *group* tourists. However, in terms of PPEI per day groups from Malaysia and China generate the most. Taking the whole year in aggregate, American and Chinese *independent* market segments contribute the largest amount of PPEI.

The results showed how types of spending, and the supply-chains, can affect net impact on the poor. For example, while Korean tourists were one of the largest markets in terms of volume but generated low PPEI per visit because they tend not to visit secondary destinations and their expenditure on shopping, although relatively high, tends not to be on items that generate income for the poor.

In general, tourists who spent less per day tended to stay longer and vice versa. Japanese tourists were only medium generators of PPEI in total. However, this was because they tended to make short visits even though the PPEI they generated per day was high. Therefore, a policy of encouraging Japanese tourists to stay an extra night would yield relatively high returns in terms of impact on PPEI.

1.5.4 Recognising Tourism Assets

When considering a destination's future potential, recognition and assessment of its tourism assets is as important as an understanding of markets. The two are, of course, related as assets are only of real tourism value if they are relevant to markets, and the range of assets in a destination will partly determine its appeal to different markets.

In general, the main assets of a destination, in terms of its ability to attract tourists, include:

- location and transport – good accessibility to tourist flows and sources, reflecting both geographical position and quality of infrastructure such as roads;

- landscape and natural heritage – mountains, coast, wildlife, protected areas;

- built heritage – iconic buildings, attractive towns and villages;

- cultural/living heritage – traditions, arts, crafts, music, cuisine, events;

- resources (environments and facilities) for particular activities – e.g. diving, hiking, kayaking;

- existing tourism facilities – lodges, hotels, restaurants, established visitor sites and attractions;

- awareness of the destination, preferably as a recognisable brand.

---

22   Cited in Ashley and Mitchell, 2008.

The quality of these assets, and the possibility and process of relating them to markets, is of central concern to destination management.

The stock of assets is not necessarily wholly static. Some, such as transport schemes or lodge developments, may be proposed or in the pipeline, and provide a particular opportunity to design in a pro-poor approach. It is important to keep abreast of change.

A destination's tourism assets also include certain resources that are important both to the successful future development and operation of tourism and to the generation of the value that is retained in the destination. These include:

- local labour supply – amount of skilled and unskilled people that could engage in tourism;

- availability (existing and potential) of local produce for direct sale to tourists and for use in tourism facilities through local supply chains;

- availability of land, building materials, clean water and energy sources;

- social assets, such as desire of local residents to welcome tourists – openness and friendliness;

- acceptable levels of safety and security;

- stable and responsive local governance and business environment;

- availability of funding and technical capacity to take action.

A key issue for pro-poor tourism is the extent to which opportunities exist for the poor to gain from these assets and resources. Three key questions to consider are:

- Do poor households or communities have any rights of ownership (legal or traditional) over some of these assets, which will enable them to gain benefit from them?

- Do poor communities depend on certain of these assets for their livelihood and wellbeing? This may restrict the use of these resources for tourism or underline the need to very careful control and management of their use.

- What potential is there for the poor to participate in presenting these assets to tourists or providing resources to the tourism industry? The many detailed issues raised by this question are covered in looking at the seven mechanisms in part 2.

There are no particular rules by which to assess a destination's assets and their implications for the poor. However, involving the full range of stakeholders as identified in 1.3, each bringing their particular knowledge and insights to the process, will help to ensure that the full range of assets is identified and assessed.

Some further guidance on identifying particular assets which may be turned into specific tourist products by poor communities is contained in Annex 3-A.

1.5.5 Considering Resource Constraints and Limiting Factors

Consideration of future tourism potential should also pay attention to aspects of the destination which may limit the possibilities for successful tourism development or for tourism to benefit the poor.

Many constraints and limiting factors will be the obverse of one of the tourism assets. For example:

- difficulty of access;

- lack of features of inherent visitor appeal;

- absence of infrastructure and existing facilities (e.g. roads, communications);

- lack of land, water, energy sources;

- a population not keen to welcome visitors;

- perceived lack of safety and security;

- sources of labour, produce etc not well suited to the sector;

- weak local supply chains;

- weak governance, limited knowledge and capacity and lack of funding;

- competing activities that may threaten tourism economically or environmentally (e.g. mining).

These factors may prohibit all tourism development or restrict the destination's potential just in certain markets or for certain types of product.

Further consideration should also be given to the possibility that certain types of tourism development or activity may actually harm the wellbeing of the poor and exacerbate rather than alleviate poverty in the short or long term. This could occur through:

- removing or depleting precious life-supporting resources;

- devaluing and eroding cultural heritage;

- bringing environmental pollution;

- destroying social structures in communities;

- diverting resources from other livelihood strategies which may offer greater stability, and introducing economic vulnerability.

As with tourism assets, consideration of constraints and limiting factors should be based on careful assessment and widespread consultation with stakeholders, especially local communities.

Further guidance on considering the impact of tourism on local livelihoods in an integrated way is contained in Annex 1, which was also referred to in section 1.3.

1.5.6 Paying Attention to Other Destinations

When considering the future potential of a destination, in terms of markets, assets and constraints, it is important to look closely at what other destinations are offering. There are three main reasons for this:

- **To learn from the experience of others.** Try to build up a regular exchange with other destinations elsewhere in the same country. Seek help from NGOs and development assistance agencies in making contact with similar destinations elsewhere. If appropriate, set up a study tour for stakeholders.

- **To size up the competition.** In recent years many new destinations have emerged, especially in the field of cultural, rural and activity tourism. It is important to be realistic about how any one destination stacks up against others, internationally and particularly within the same country. The choice of target markets and development strategies should take account of the competition in particular markets and products. The unique selling points (USPs) of the destination should be identified. Wherever possible, opportunities should be pursued to establish a distinctive brand and product offer, provided that they can be shown both to be in line with market requirements and to offer benefits to the poor.

- **To identify opportunities for future collaboration.** Other destinations should be seen as potential collaborators and partners as well as competitors. By working together destinations can combine assets and resources to mutual advantage.

Take time to scrutinise a wide range of marketing material and build up contacts. Keeping in touch with other destinations should occur as an ongoing process not just in the planning and assessment stages.

1.5.7 Summarising the Situation

A useful way of summarising the assessment of the destination's potential, and agreeing and sharing it with others, is to present it as a simple analysis of strengths, weaknesses, opportunities and threats (SWOT).

A SWOT analysis starts by writing down a particular goal – in this case "to achieve poverty alleviation through tourism". Under this list the destination's strengths and weaknesses and the perceived opportunities and threats, as short bullet points in a template as shown in table 3 below.

Strengths and weakness are **internal** factors and will include the destination's assets, resources and limitations as they currently exist. These are factors which are within the control of the destination's stakeholders, which have a chance to influence or change them.

Opportunities and threats relate to the future and are **external** factors and include market trends and changing circumstances such as global security. These are factors which are beyond the control of the destination's stakeholders but should be taken into account by them. It is important to remember that 'opportunities' concerns context and circumstances – don't use this box to list possible actions.

In order to achieve the goal, strengths need to be maintained and used, weaknesses remedied, opportunities exploited and threats assessed and planned for.

Table 3   SWOT template – showing examples of types of factors to include

Goal: To achieve poverty alleviation through tourism		
	Positive Helpful to achieving the goal	**Negative** Harmful to achieving the goal
Internal Current. Mainly open to control and influence	**Strengths** • Key assets • Available resources • Comparative advantages over competition	**Weaknesses** • Gaps in, or quality of, assets • Resource constraints • Process or funding challenges • Comparative disadvantages
External For future. Mainly beyond direct control	**Opportunities** • Key markets and market trends • Technological advances • Other destinations seeking partners	**Threats** • Political and economic instability • Climate change (sometimes an opportunity) • Strengthening competitors

1.5 Considering market opportunities, assets and constraints

1 Think about the types of visitor who are already coming to your destination.

   – What do you know about them – interests, needs, spending, etc.?

   – How can you find out more about them?

   – Could your destination attract more of these visitors, or get them to stay longer or spend more? What new or improved products may be necessary to achieve this?

2 Think about residents and visitors in the country who may not be coming to your destination. Which ones could you attract? Ask the same questions as above about them.

3 Bearing in mind these markets, consider your destination's main assets and resources for tourism in the future. Do any offer particular benefits for the poor?

4 Think about the main constraints and limitations for the future. Consider:

   – Lack or weakness of assets, which restrict the appeal of the destination to certain markets.

   – Resource issues, which might affect the ability of the destination to develop tourism and future impacts on the poor.

5 Think about other destinations in the country and elsewhere. Which ones do you see as your main competitors? What can you learn from them? Which ones might you work with?

6 Summarise your answers by filling in a SWOT table for the destination. Bear in mind any other internal and external factors that are relevant to the destination and to poverty alleviation that you may not have considered above.

1.6 Agreeing on a Strategy and Action Plan to Alleviate Poverty Through Tourism

The steps taken so far will have enabled the set of stakeholders working together in the destination to have:

•   gained an understanding of poverty there and identified targets for its alleviation;

•   understood how tourism is functioning, how and to what extent the poor benefit and where this might be improved;

•   considered future market and resource opportunities and constraints and implications for the poor.

It is now time to use this evidence to agree on a way forward and plan some action.

1.6.1 Preparing a Comprehensive Strategy for Sustainable Tourism

In line with the integrated approach advocated throughout this manual, rather than producing separate destination management and pro-poor tourism strategies, it is suggested that a single tourism strategy and action plan (which may be called a destination management plan) is prepared.

As with the evidence gathering preceding it, this should be a participatory process involving considerable consultation with all stakeholders.

Typically, tourism strategies cover a five year period with action plans drawn up annually or spanning three years.

The strategy should be based on the principles of **sustainable tourism.** These principles and their implications for tourism strategy formulation have been looked at in detail elsewhere.[23] Essentially, they require that the strategy should lead to the development of tourism which is:

- **Economically viable and competitive,** delivering local prosperity and employment which can be maintained over time.

- **Socially equitable and culturally sensitive,** benefiting the poor and disadvantaged groups and enhancing cultural richness and quality of life.

- **Environmentally responsible,** minimising global and local pollution and conserving natural resources and biodiversity.

The strategy should identify **aims** for tourism in the destination which reflect these principles.

The strategy and action plan should not only focus on poverty alleviation. However, one of the primary aims articulated in the strategy should be specifically directed at this goal. This might be expressed as:

To contribute to the alleviation of poverty in [name of destination] by securing a significant increase in the flow of income and opportunities to the poor.

The presence of the specific poverty alleviation aim, as one of the key aims for tourism, should:

- Profoundly influence the overall shape and direction of tourism in the destination;

- Drive a set of actions designed specifically to deliver benefits from tourism for the poor.

This aim should sit alongside other primary or subsidiary aims which may be directed at other economic, social and environmental priorities.

Many of these other aims are likely also to be important in improving the wellbeing of the poor.[24] They might include aims, leading to related actions, to:

- **Increase the amount of spending by tourists in the destination.** The overall volume of spending will affect the level of income received by the poor.

- **Improve the performance and profitability of local tourism businesses.** This can be an essential prerequisite for securing and maintaining benefits from tourism.

- **Increase inward investment in tourism.** This may be critical in growing the size of the tourism economy and its overall impact on poverty.

- **Reduce the impact of tourism on the local environment and resources.** Certain forms of tourism may be restricting the availability for poor communities of key resources such water, land, natural materials and valuable habitats.

The full set of aims should be reflected in a short **vision statement** for sustainable tourism. This should describe the performance and contribution of tourism in the destination in five years time.

1.6.2 Making Strategic Choices from a Pro-poor Perspective

The strategic part of the strategy and action plan should show how the vision will be attained. It will set a direction for tourism as a whole and so must be appropriate and meaningful for general tourism planning and provide the basis for a tourism sector that is competitive and sustainable but also pro-poor. This will involve making some strategic choices.

---

23   World Tourism Organization, 2005.

24   Many of these aims may be directed at increasing the size of the tourism economy (size of the cake) rather than focussing on reaching the poor *per se* (shares of the cake) – see pag 5.

Some of the main strategic choices are shown in table 4, together with the related questions to address from a pro-poor perspective. The evidence gathered during the processes outlined in sections 1.3, 1.4 and 1.5 should enable choices to be made which are appropriate to the destination.

Table 4   Strategic choices and questions from a pro-poor perspective

Strategic choices	Questions to address
The position and relative priority given to tourism in the sustainable development of the destination	• How is tourism performing compared with other economic sectors and livelihood enhancement scenarios? • What alternative options exist for economic growth and poverty alleviation? • Is a focus on tourism justified – should it be stepped up? • Is there a danger of over-dependence on tourism? • Can the integration of tourism with other sectors be improved? • Is tourism, or aspects of it, actually exacerbating poverty – e.g. through depleting resources? • Should the volume of tourism, or some elements of it, be reduced?
The attention given to environmental and socio-cultural impacts	• How serious are environmental and resource use issues in the destination? • How serious are social-cultural issues in the destination? • Can these be addressed by better management of tourism? • Do they restrict the kind of tourism that should be developed?
The degree of focus on particular beneficiaries	• Who should be the main beneficiaries of tourism? • What priority should be given to the poor? • Should priority be given to achieving a volumetric change in poverty levels across the whole destination or to bringing benefit to particular communities? • Should there be a focus on women, certain minorities and disadvantaged groups?
The geographical distribution of tourism in the destination	• Should priority areas and sites for tourism development be identified within the destination? If so, which? • Should attempts be made to bring tourism income/benefit, directly or indirectly, to remote communities?
The selection of target markets	• Which markets are currently delivering the most tourism income in the destination? • Which show greatest potential for growth? • Are these markets also effective in generating spending that reaches the poor (see criteria in section 1.5) or would others be better?
The selection of priority products	• Which current tourism products appear to be delivering most benefit to the poor? • Are these products attractive to the target markets – can they be developed and promoted further? • Can these products be made to be more pro-poor? • Are there other existing products and activities that could be made to be more pro-poor? • What kind of new products and activities can be developed that are good at delivering benefit to the poor?
The setting of targets	• What is a realistic target for the volume of visitors and spending in the destination in five years time? • What is a realistic target for the number of poor households receiving a significant increase in annual income in five years time, and/or having their wellbeing enhanced in other ways, due to tourism (see part 3)?

1.6.3 Identifying and Prioritising Interventions

As well as setting a shape for tourism in the destination, the strategy should provide the basis for identifying and prioritising interventions.

Interventions driven wholly or partly by the poverty alleviation aim should seek to generate higher levels of income and wellbeing for the poor, as a result of expenditure of tourists and tourism enterprises or investments associated with the sector.

There are three main ways to bring this about, expressed in these three **objectives:**

1   To increase the overall volume of spending – primary spending by tourists and secondary spending by tourism enterprises (i.e. the economic flow in the tourism value chain).

2   To increase the proportion of spending that reaches the poor, through:

   – increasing participation levels by the poor;

   – strengthening channels for spending by tourists to reach the poor;

   – strengthening the relative profile of pro-poor products and enterprises in the destination.

3   To increase tourism related investment that has direct and/or spin-off benefits for the poor.

The above forms of intervention are not mutually exclusive and should be pursued alongside each other.

One way of increasing the volume of spending (objective 1) and investment (objective 3) may simply be to seek to raise the volume of tourism as a whole in the destination. This could be achieved through more effective and active destination marketing and through general investment promotion. This should be addressed in the strategy and action plan.

However, more targeted interventions are also necessary, combining the three objectives and focusing on particular products and markets. These should also be expressed in the strategy and action plan. The approach, illustrated in figure 4, is to:

- Work with products (A) which may be generating high volumes of spending to try to raise the proportion of that spending which reaches the poor. An example might be a resort or business hotel.

- Work with products (B) which may already be delivering a high proportion of spending to the poor, to increase their viability, net size and the volume of spending on them. An example may be a community-based tourism initiative.

- Foster, support and encourage growth and ever greater participation of the poor in products (C) which are already receiving a significant volume of spending with a high proportion of this being already channelled to the poor. An example may be a successful eco-lodge or local tour operation with a strong private operator-community relationship.

The approach should not only relate to existing products. New products should be encouraged, ideally of type (C) but possibly of types (A) or (B) provided actions are put in place for their further growth and transformation. Any new developments encouraged should be able to demonstrate an ability to appeal to, and reach, the selected target markets.

Figure 4   Pro-poor growth model

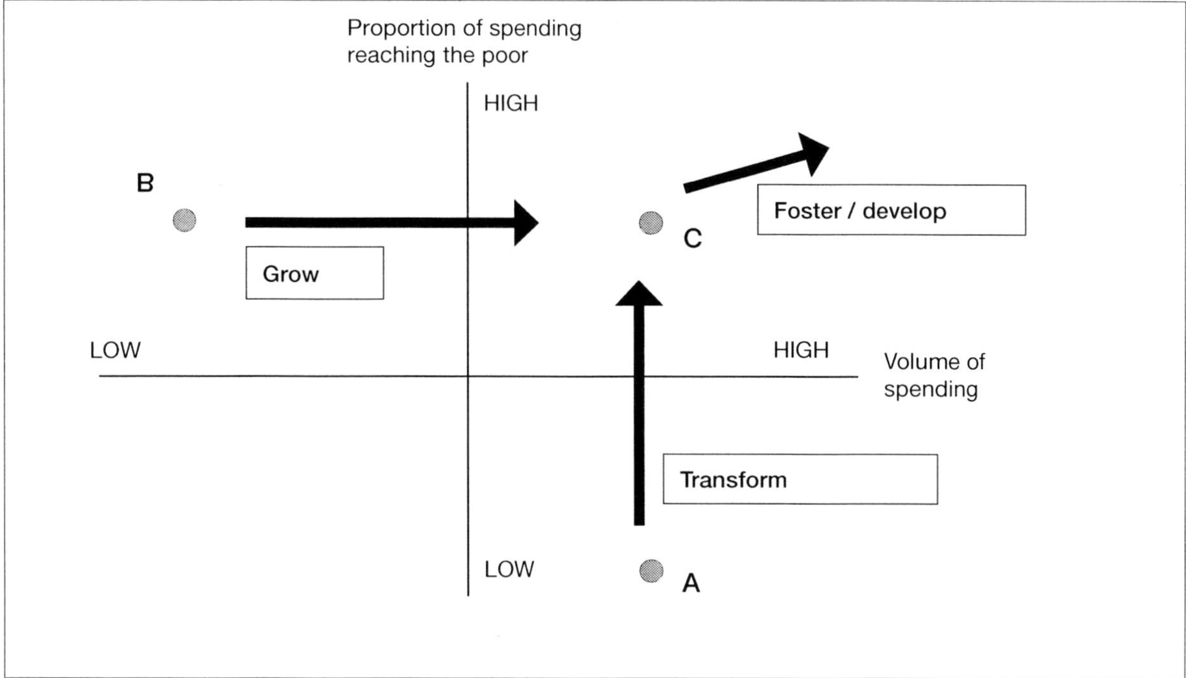

1.6.4 Working up Interventions

Designing specific interventions based around the above model requires further choices to be made about where exactly to intervene. The value chain analysis (section 1.4) combined with the market, asset and SWOT analysis (section 1.5) will help here. Special attention should also be paid to the choice between product development and market development as described in the Ansoff Matrix model in section 1.5. These considerations should be used to identify the products and markets on which to focus.

Products may be taken as: packages, such as safari excursions; types of experience, such as village visits; types of enterprise, such as lodges or craft retailers; or individual enterprises. In the example from Northern Tanzania (box 5, p. 22) the Kilimanjaro 'product' was compared with the Safari 'product', finding that, in terms of total revenue reaching poor, the latter had a greater impact and might therefore been seen as a potential focus for action.

It is also important to consider individual elements or **components** of products which may be performing more or less well in securing benefits for the poor. These components may relate to particular services, spending opportunities or elements of the supply chain. In the analysis of the Kilimanjaro trek the great importance of porters' wages and tips was identified, which is an element that needs to be maintained and fostered, while the relatively low pro-poor benefit obtained from the high expenditure on park fees suggests that this is a component requiring some transformation. In another example, from Laos,[25] it was found that the greatest potential for expanding pro-poor impact of crafts in Luang Prabang does not come from further expansion of sales but from increasing the share of silk that comes from poor farmers.

Consideration should be given to the **starting point** for interventions. The individual circumstances of different destinations may dictate whether it is more appropriate to design interventions:

- around the poor – e.g. working with individual communities to identify and pursue opportunities for them to participate in tourism or indirectly benefit from it; or

- around the industry – e.g. working with particular private sector enterprises to strengthen their links to the poor.

25   Ashley, 2006b.

In both cases, it will be important to identify and address the **barriers** to initial participation. This will involve understanding perceptions, practical problems and other factors which may be holding back the poor on the one hand and tourism enterprises on the other. Processes relating to intervention with communities and the private sector are further discussed in section 1.7.

It is important to recognise that many of the interventions covered in the strategy and action plan will be concerned with broad issues of destination management. These will have a strong bearing on the overall success of tourism in the destination and hence on the chances of alleviating poverty. Examples of these interventions include:

- **Strengthening infrastructure and communications.** As well as benefiting tourism, this can directly help poor communities and open opportunities in all sectors.

- **Improving awareness and brand positioning of the destination in selected markets.** As a subsidiary aim, this can be crucial in achieving necessary visitor flows and spending.

- **Improving visitor information and the interpretation of cultural heritage.** As well as improving the overall quality of experience, this can play a major role in influencing visitor behaviour and the level of spending directed to the poor.

- **Improving safety and security.** This can be an major barrier for tourism in some destinations and addressing it would also benefit poor communities.

Technical guidance on these management and marketing actions is not contained in this manual and can be found elsewhere.[26]

Other interventions will be more focussed on **specific actions to channel tourism benefits to the poor.** The opportunities for this are looked at in detail in part 2 of this manual. It is important to review these before selecting the interventions to pursue.

1.6.5 Creating an Action Plan

The answers to strategic questions and the approach to interventions should form the basis for drawing up the action plan.

This should for the final part of the strategy and action plan document, but also be separate from it so it can be regularly reviewed and updated. It may be written as a one, two or three year plan, depending on what is most appropriate for the destination. It should specify actions to be taken by different stakeholders, individually or jointly, and which may be coordinated by the DM group.

A long list of possible actions may be drawn up initially, which should then be filtered down to a small, manageable list. In weighing up actions from a pro-poor perspective, both the impact on poverty and the practicability of the action should be considered.

Considerations of impact should include:

- the number of people in poverty who will be reached by the action;

- the likely increase in income per person reached;

- any non-financial benefits that could reach the poor;

- the ability of the action to reach the particular target segment of those in poverty;

- the extent to which measurement of the action's impact is possible;

- speed and visibility of impact – important for building interest and confidence;

---

26   E.g. World Tourism Organization, 2007.

- the sustainability of results – how long will they last and will they need continuing support?

- the extent to which the action will enhance knowledge and can be replicated.

Considerations of practicality should include:

- the cost of the action;

- possible funding and other resources available;

- relevance to agreed policies and commitments;

- the availability of people with sufficient capacity to carry it out;

- the chance of success and the risk implications.

1.6.6 Taking a Pragmatic Approach

The above provides a comprehensive guide to a systematic process of drawing up a tourism strategy and action plan for the destination which includes poverty alleviation as a primary aim. In practice it may not be possible to follow such a considered path. It is important not to spend too much time and effort on reflection and analysis at the expense of actually taking action. Much will depend on the resources available and on the interests and commitment of the different stakeholders. Often action will be dictated by opportunities that arise. However, it is always important to be able to justify and prioritise actions against a logical view of their relevance in meeting ultimate aims and objectives.

This can be an iterative process. Destinations that move swiftly towards actions can learn from the experience while also taking time to develop a more structured and planned approach for the future.

Box 8 Inhambane, Mozambique – Integrated Tourism Development[27]

The Integrated Tourism Development Project, in the destination of Inhambane, north of Maputo provides an example of the many destinations that have started to adopt a comprehensive and integrated approach to destination management with a focus on poverty alleviation. While not fully addressing all the steps outlined in this manual, it has reflected a number of them and is revisiting them as part of an ongoing process.

Rather than developing a detailed strategy and action plan, it has begun to take early action but based on relevant analysis. It's approach has been to 'concentrate on short term win-win activities while a longer term programme is being developed and as the actors gain more confidence, capacity and interest'. This pragmatic, iterative approach may also be relevant elsewhere.

The project has brought together 16 key actors – public, private and NGOs who network together. This has replaced a previous total lack of collaboration. The Provincial Tourism Operators Association has been re-formed and is beginning to coordinate private sector enterprises. On the public sector side, the Municipal Council has begun to appreciate its role in tourism and in the need to relate this to basic services such as garbage cleaning. A DMO has not yet been formed, but sensitisation towards this has taken place.

A detailed baseline study of tourism was undertaken. This was able to identify the significance of direct employment in tourism compared with a weak local supply chain with poor links to agriculture. Basic assessment of different market segments was undertaken, concluding that South African self-catering tourists spent little in the area and the greatest potential lay in servicing high-end hotels through stimulating local employment and developing the supply chain.

Actions towards this end have included:

- training local people in hospitality and basic tourism skills;

- developing a pilot project to link vegetable and fruit producers to tourism;

- diversifying the product, with a stronger cultural offer – establishing a craft market;

- improving environmental management, starting by addressing garbage.

These early, visible results based on a first cycle of the process – work together, analyse, prioritise (plan), act – will help to underpin further cycles, leading to stronger partnership, sounder planning and more confident action in future.

1.6 Assessing the need for a new a strategy and action plan and steps to take

1 Consider reasons why having a robust strategy and action plan may be helpful in your aim to alleviate poverty. These may include external and internal relationships – winning support and funding, allocating resources effectively and maintaining commitment over time.

2 Think whether there is an existing tourism strategy and action plan for the destination, or any kind of document or general agreement on aims, objectives and interventions in tourism.

   – If yes: Is it based on sustainability principles? Does it include poverty alleviation as a major aim? Does it reflect the kinds of analysis outlined here and form a good basis for pro-poor interventions – or can it be made to do so?

   – If no: Can such a strategy and action plan be created? Who will need to come together to do this? Will outside help be necessary?

3 Think about the amount of time you will need to prepare a strategy and action plan. Can you sustain interest during this period? Do you need to take actions quickly? Can you relate and modify existing actions around the development of a plan and use them to inform future planning?

1.7 Strengthening Stakeholder Response and Capacity

Actions will require participation by different stakeholders who may need to be encouraged and helped to deliver them. This section considers the situation of three main groups of stakeholders: private sector enterprises; communities; and supporting institutions.

1.7.1 Influencing the Private Sector

Engagement of private sector enterprises, large and small, and encouraging them to take action to assist in poverty alleviation is fundamentally important. All of the mechanisms for channelling tourism spending towards the poor, covered in part 2, require their participation. Indeed, private sector businesses often provide a good starting point for new initiatives.

Contact with private enterprises could entail:

- **Responding to their own initiatives.** Pro-poor actions may well be started independently by an enterprise owner or operator, who should then be offered support by the public sector and other stakeholders.

- **Working through the DM group, enterprise networks or high profile, well respected individual enterprises.** Exerting collective or peer pressure can be an effective way forward. This was referred to in section 1.2.

- **Approaching enterprises before development occurs.** This may be a good time to seek to exert influence, possibly helped through some of the tools mentioned below.

Private sector tourism enterprises and networks are increasingly showing concern about poverty issues and taking relevant action, often for deep seated altruistic reasons but also because they recognise the benefits that can be achieved for their businesses. Many international tour operators are now requiring the enterprises they work with to demonstrate a positive approach to local communities and are in turn pointing this out to their clients.

It is extremely important to emphasise the following benefits of engaging in pro-poor actions, when seeking to influence businesses:

- **Winning positive public relations benefits with investors, business partners and consumers.** This can occur through the enterprise's own publicity to tourists, through its Corporate Social Responsibility (CSR) reporting to the commercial and public sectors, and through opportunities to gain positive media coverage.

- **Generating good relations with staff.** This can lead to business advantages through quality of performance, loyalty and reduced staff turnover and creating a happy atmosphere for customers.

- **Securing good relations with neighbouring communities.** This is important for developing linkages in the supply chain and labour market but also for such issues as security and the appearance and conservation of the local environment.

- **Obtaining direct economic benefits.** A number of pro-poor actions can generate direct economic benefit, such as reducing transport costs by shortening supply chains and working with poor communities to develop complementary products than can be promoted to guests.

These factors may be sufficient to win private sector engagement in poverty alleviation. However, a number of specific policy tools[28] can be used to influence the private sector. These should be borne in mind when promoting the actions outlined in part 2.

Regulatory tools

- Introducing obligatory practices and standards that are backed by regulation and legislation.

- Placing conditions on enterprises seeking permission for development or a license to operate. This can include, for example, requiring private enterprises to support local communities when granting a concession to operate in a protected area. See example in box 9.

Economic tools

- Providing direct financial assistance to support certain actions (e.g. incentives, donations, grants or loans).

- Making the presence of pro-poor practices (e.g. in employment or procurement) a necessary condition of receiving financial assistance or qualifying for tax exemption.

---

28   More detail on these tools can be found in World Tourism Organization, 2005.

Voluntary tools

- Providing and promoting guidelines and codes of conduct on good and bad practice.

- Establishing and promoting certification schemes[29] that set out requirements for enterprises, verify that they have been met, and award a label in recognition. See example in box 10.

- Encouraging CSR reporting by all enterprises.

- Publicising and rewarding particularly good practice, as an example to others and as a way of giving exposure to those enterprises making a significant contribution to poverty alleviation.

Supportive tools

- Assisting enterprises, especially small businesses, to build their capacity to deliver benefits to the poor, through relevant advice and training – see below.

- Helping enterprises that are following good practice with their marketing, including providing a promotional platform for them.

Box 9 Granting concessions in South African National Parks[30]

In the year 2000 South African National Parks (SANParks) introduced a Commercialisation Strategy in order to reduce dependency on state funding and to improve existing operational efficiencies. This resulted in the awarding of concession sites to 11 private accommodation operators, 17 restaurants and 21 shops. A typical concession allows the operators to build and operate tourism facilities with the parks on the basis of a 20 year contract in return for the payment of a fee. Against these rights of occupation and commercial use, there is a set of obligations on the concessionaire regarding financial terms, environmental management, social objectives, empowerment and other factors. Infringement of these carries specified penalties, underpinned by performance bonds and finally termination of the contract.

The exercise has been successful, with significant commercial gains (over £15m net received from concession fees and rentals in 2007) and considerable improvements in the quality of the visitor experience, environmental impact and the image of SANParks. However, one of the most positive benefits has been in socio-economic development. The Private Party agreements signed to meet the obligations on the concessionaires have resulted in commitments generating: 620 new jobs (excluding construction); 79% of employees from poor communities adjacent to the parks; guaranteed spend of US$ 1.6 million per annum in the local communities; and considerable transfer of skills.

---

29 In order to strengthen voluntary processes, Global Sustainable Tourism Criteria have been prepared by a working group of international bodies, to provide common standards for use by enterprises, destinations and certification schemes. See (www.sustainabletourismcriteria.org) (1-11-2009).

30 Varghese, 2008.

Box 10 An example of certification[31]

Fair Trade in Tourism South Africa (FTTSA) awards a certification Trademark to tourism businesses that are able to demonstrate commitment to a set of principles and compliance with predetermined criteria. FTTSA concentrates on social issues, although concern for the environment and use of resources is also taken into account. The 13 operational areas covered by the certification are: Legal and general; Labour standards; Human resources; Skills development; Employment equity; Ownership; Procurement; Community; Environment and conservation; Health and safety; Quality and reliability; Workplace culture, and HIV/Aids policy.

The Trademark is awarded on the basis of self-assessment followed by external verification. It relates closely to the responsible tourism policy and guidelines of the South African government, whose endorsement has been important to its credibility. The main motivation and benefits seen by those awarded the Trademark have been the opportunity for increased awareness, improved access to niche markets, networking, exchange of knowledge, mutual support and benchmarking between them.

Capacity building activities, primarily in the form of technical advice and training, may be directed in two ways, at:

- **General performance of the business.** Many service enterprises in developing countries are small or micro enterprises – SMEs[32]. Inability to deliver benefits to the poor may relate generally to their weak trading position and overall lack of knowledge and skills. Some may be established by the poor themselves (see section 2.4 below). Capacity building should cover business training, hospitality skills, market knowledge and marketing.

- **Strengthening pro-poor activities.** This could relate to all kinds of enterprise, large and small. It should cover the various matters that come up in part 2 such as recruitment practice, supply chain management, community relationships etc. It may be geared to particular levels of management, for example sessions aimed at chefs and procurement staff on supply chains.

Experience of training delivered in this context has highlighted the importance of:

- being absolutely clear about the needs of the enterprises and the level they are at – tailoring delivery around this;

- making sure the right people attend who can actually implement what is learnt;

- keeping training sessions short, so they can be fitted into work requirements;

- selecting locations carefully;

- employing trainers with both technical and communication skills and who can build a rapport with the audience and win their confidence;

- using communication techniques, including language, appropriate to the audience;

- providing incentives to attend if necessary, without creating dependency;

- linking training into processes of self-assessment and future learning and support.

---

31   From World Tourism Organization, 2005 and (www.fairtourismsa.org.za) (1-11-2009).

32   The term SME is sometimes used for 'small and medium sized enterprises'. In this context of this document, the micro level (smallest of all) is more relevant than the medium.

Box 11 Promoting Inclusive Businesses[33]

SNV has been promoting the concept of 'inclusive businesses'. This term stands for businesses that are sustainable, are successful in business terms and also benefit low-income communities. It is increasingly working with individual tourism enterprises or associations to guide and support them in making their activities pro-poor. This includes strengthening their access to markets.

In Nepal the **Marketing Assistance for Sustainable Tourism Products project (MAST),** implemented by UNEP, SNV and the Nepal Tourism Board, supported Nepali tourism businesses to integrate pro-poor sustainable tourism principles and practices into their business operations and to market their sustainable tourism products by providing necessary tools, skills and support through its capacity building programme. In its approach, the project sought to reward those companies which could clearly demonstrate implementation of sustainable practices and provide a clear business incentive to others to embrace sustainable business practices.

Outcomes included: enhanced understanding of pro-poor principles among participating companies; increased linkages between businesses and local communities for the provision of products and services; and increased gender diversity practices. Within a very short period, a significant number of new (national and international) business partnerships were created bringing new businesses to these companies.

Lessons learned were:

- tailor trainings to the needs of the businesses - provide short, sharp, practical training sessions and address the lack of basic business skills among many tourism entrepreneurs;

- use of industry trainers and success stories;

- provide on-going mentoring and support for participating companies and develop simple, practical, self-help resources;

- provide increased incentives for adherence to responsible pro-poor business practice.

Building on the lessons learned from the MAST-Nepal project, SNV Nepal initiated the **Responsible Travel Nepal** Programme with the aim to up-scale MAST-Nepal best practices and encourage and reward more responsible social and environmental practices in Nepal's tourism industry.

1.7.2 Working with Communities

The capacity of the poor to respond to opportunities clearly affects the potential for poverty alleviation through tourism. Specific actions to take to develop opportunities for the poor and to support them are covered in detail under the individual mechanisms described in part 2. However, it is important to consider generic processes to engage poor communities at the outset and to help them assess how tourism might contribute to their livelihood.

Key outcomes should be:

- Awareness – simply helping communities understand who tourists are, what they are looking for, how to interact with them, and some of the positive and negative issues associated with tourism.

- Realism – an appreciation of what tourism can and cannot offer and the chances of success in the community, avoiding unrealistic expectations.

- Empowerment – ensuring that communities are in a position to determine their own future engagement in tourism and to make well informed decisions.

---

33   From SNV Nepal.

A number of models have been developed from experience, which are particularly appropriate for working with communities – villages, indigenous groups etc. – rather than with individuals. The approach involves a structured participation processes, working with local people to help them identify assets, needs, aspirations and achievable actions. An example is given in box 12.

Where appropriate, these kinds of approaches could be adopted with individual communities within the destination. However, it is important to think carefully about this before embarking on activity that it may not be possible to follow through successfully. This should include:

- Putting an emphasis on realistically assessing tourism potential with the communities – for many, tourism may offer little benefit or not be appropriate.

- Paying particular attention to potential market response and the practicality of communication with markets, at the outset and throughout the process. The communities will need good guidance to ensure that any plan meets a demand from tourists. Tour operator and other private sector involvement can help in this respect.

- Considering the future needs of communities in terms of ongoing support and whether this can be delivered.

- Looking at relationships between communities and the private sector as a particular way forward.

In some destinations there may already be projects working with communities on sustainable development, which could look at tourism as an opportunity alongside other livelihood options. This could provide a sensible starting point.

Further details on community-based tourism initiatives and community-private sector partnerships are provided in section 2.4.

Box 12 Appreciative Participatory Planning and Action – Nepal[34]

The Tourism for Rural Poverty Alleviation Programme (TRPAP) in Nepal used the Appreciative Participatory Planning and Action (APPA) model in social mobilisation, in planning and in the implementation of activities when working with communities. APPA allows communities and groups to identify and emphasise their successes and strengths as a means to empower them, so that they can manage their own development and make use of valuable local knowledge and skills.

Facilitators spent time in each community, building a rapport with them. They then initiated a three day tourism planning exercise, involving 20 to 30 members of the community, based on the APPA model. The approach makes use of a 5-D cycle:

- Discovery – identifies strengths and successes.

- Dream – images of the community's future.

- Direction – marks out the future.

- Design – plans the future.

- Delivery – sustains the action and reflects on achievements.

Through APPA, plans were made to assess the feasibility of 'producing and marketing' pro-poor sustainable tourism activities such as guided village tours or forest walks, and an action plan was developed to generate local benefits from it.

---

34   From SNV Nepal, 2004 and 2006.

Lessons learned included paying attention to: linkages between key stakeholders; co-ordination between micro and macro-level; abilities of community groups and the private sector to exploit economic opportunities; and proactive marketing.

By the end of the project, over 360 APPA workshops covering over 66% of the total households had been conducted in the programme areas. More than 635 Community Organizations were made capable of managing their institutions and performing regular functions like bookkeeping and communication as well as participatory decision making. Altogether, over 7,400 local stakeholders were trained to provide various tourism related services.

1.7.3 Strengthening Institutions

In any destination, a number of institutions (public sector bodies, NGOs and private sector groupings or representative bodies) will be involved in implementing the tourism strategy and taking pro-poor action. These have been described in section 1.2. Many may need help in fulfilling their role.

Advice and training for these institutions should focus on three main areas:

- General tourism knowledge. Experience from many developing countries suggests that basic technical knowledge on the functioning of the tourism sector can be quite limited at a local destination level, including amongst government officials and NGOs.

- Specific knowledge relating tourism and poverty alleviation. This relates to the subjects covered in this manual.

- Organizational development. Capacity to deliver may be hampered by internal and external management issues, requiring assistance with resource mobilisation, organizational development and communication. This may apply particularly to networking bodies perhaps established specifically for the purpose of coordinating private stakeholders, rather than more established NGOs.

A series of training courses should be developed, tailored to the needs of the institutions, including sessions based around the material in this manual. Such training sessions could be used as a way of bringing bodies together and help to secure future commitment to joint working.

In section 1.2, the establishment of some kind of loose destination management (DM) group was advocated. The degree of formalisation of such a structure will depend on what is appropriate for the destination at the time. However, it may well be helpful to set up some institutional strengthening, particularly in the field of organizational development referred to above, for this DM group, possibly leading on to a fully fledged Destination Management Organisation. In part 2, much of the content refers to actions that can be taken by the DM group, leading and coordinating the different stakeholders.

 **1.7 Considering stakeholders' needs and how to influence and support them**

1   Do you think that the private sector enterprises in your destination are aware of the positive advantages to them of working with local communities and providing opportunities for the poor? What messages need to be strengthened?

2   Think about the list of tools that could be used to stimulate a response from private enterprises.

   – Are any of them already being used?

   – Which ones do you think are most relevant in your area?

3   Do you think that it is necessary to provide more training and capacity building to tourism enterprises to support general tourism business performance as well as pro-poor approaches? Is this happening already and can it be strengthened?

4   Are there any structured programmes of capacity building on sustainable development with individual communities at the moment, which may or may not include tourism? Is there scope to introduce tourism programmes with communities, with a realistic chance of success? What priority should be given to this?

5   Which institutional bodies, groups and partners do you feel are in particular need of more capacity building? Are their needs the same and what are they? How do you think they can best me met?

6   In section 1.2 you were encouraged to think about coordination mechanisms and structures in your destination and what would work best for you. What help do you feel that this structure will need, now and in the future, to ensure its success?

Taking Action –
Mechanisms for Reaching the Poor

Part 1 of this manual looked at structures and processes for analysing and planning tourism in a destination and how they are affected by a focus on poverty alleviation. It proposed the establishment of a tourism strategy and action plan (or destination management plan) based on this analysis which embraces pro-poor concerns and actions.

Many actions identified in the destination's tourism strategy and action plan will be aimed at developing and marketing the product. By bringing more tourism spending into the destination such actions may benefit the poor. However, in order to ensure that the poor stand to benefit from tourism growth, or to gain more from existing levels of tourism in the destination, it will be necessary to ensure that a set of mechanisms are in place that channel tourism spending and other tourism benefits specifically towards the poor.

This part of the manual looks in detail at these mechanisms. It takes as its basis the seven mechanisms for poverty alleviation through tourism previously identified by UNWTO[1] and used by them and SNV in developing actions in the ST-EP Programme.

The mechanisms include:

1   Employment of the poor in tourism enterprises.

2   Supply of goods and services to tourism enterprises by the poor.

3   Informal selling of goods and services to tourists by the poor.

4   Developing small/micro or community-based tourism enterprises or joint ventures.

5   Tax or charge on tourists or enterprises with proceeds benefiting the poor.

6   Voluntary giving by tourists or tourism enterprises that benefits the poor.

7   Collateral benefits to the poor from tourism investment and activity.

Comparing the mechanisms

It is important to appreciate that these mechanisms are not mutually exclusive and can be added together and support each other. They are not alternatives. Destinations and private sector enterprises should encourage and support all of them, where appropriate. Likewise, a poor household or community could benefit from a number of these mechanisms simultaneously. However, the mechanisms do vary in the way they operate and some may be more appropriate than others according to the situation.

The main players in the functioning of the mechanisms are tourists (possibly acting through the intermediary of tour operators), tourism service enterprises (such as hotels), the poor themselves, and local government or local destination management groups. NGOs may participate directly in the latter and can play an important role in influencing and supporting all the other players and all the mechanisms. Table 5 compares the mechanisms according to different roles they require from these players.

—————————————

1   In World Tourism Organization, 2004b.

Table 5   The role of different players in implementing the mechanisms

Mechanism	Service Enterprises (e.g. hotels)	Tourists and/or Tour Operators	The poor	Local government or DM group
1 Employment of the poor in tourism enterprises.	▲ Active policy of recruitment and training of poor.	Generally support relevant enterprises. Pay fair gratuities.	Look for jobs and participate in training etc.	Provide education and facilitate training and access to jobs.
2 Supply of goods and services to tourism enterprises by the poor.	▲ Active policy of auditing supply chain and sourcing from the poor.	Generally support relevant enterprises and favour local produce etc.	▲ Meet the requirements of enterprises in quality and reliability of supply.	Support suppliers and facilitate linkages and distribution channels.
3 Informal selling of goods and services to tourists by the poor.	Some facilitation – e.g. providing sales points and recommending to guests.	Be prepared to buy from poor – reduce unfair bartering etc.	▲ Provide items to meet demand at right price and quality.	▲ Organise selling, set standards and support improvements.
4 Developing small/micro or community-based tourism enterprises or joint ventures.	▲ Big variation – from no involvement, to mentoring to establishing joint venture partnerships.	Seek out and support relevant enterprises to visit or include in programmes.	▲ Major effort to establish and run enterprises effectively, with potentially high risk.	Provide the right conditions for enterprise formation and help broker partnerships.
5 Tax or charge on tourists or enterprises with proceeds benefiting the poor.	Be prepared to collect/pay the charge and meet the financial burden that this may entail.	Inform tourists of the existence and purpose of any charge .	Engage in the process to maximise receipts for the poor and ensure equitable use of the revenue.	▲ Set up and oversee tax/charge system and use revenue raised to benefit the poor.
6 Voluntary giving by tourists or tourism enterprises that benefits the poor.	Can vary between basic financial support to major engagement with communities.	▲ Requires willingness by tourists and often promotion/ organization by operators.	Receive benefit but and engage in process to ensure equitable use.	Help establish schemes and facilitate links with between recipient communities.
7 Collateral benefits to the poor from tourism investment and activity.	May depend on significant investment and adjustment of plans to meet community needs.	Operators may give some advice/ support at planning stage.	Participation in planning etc. may help to ensure tourism recognises and meets local needs.	▲ Key role in shaping and controlling tourism development to benefit the poor.

NB: The ▲ symbol indicates where a particularly key role is required from the different players in implementing and responding to the mechanism.

The seven mechanisms can be divided broadly into three groups. Mechanism 1 (employment of the poor by tourism enterprises) and Mechanism 2 (engagement of the poor in the supply chain of goods and services) essentially depend on the efforts of established (or developing) tourism enterprises, on the one hand in providing direct jobs for the poor and on the other in sourcing their supplies from them. In each case, the poor themselves need to be capable of responding to the opportunities provided by these enterprises.

Mechanisms 3 and 4 operate around purchases made by tourists from the poor. The difference between them rests mainly in the degree of organization of the poor that is entailed. Mechanism 3 is about informal selling, such as street vending, while mechanism 4 requires the setting up of a more significant enterprise or initiative by the poor, possibly as a community venture. The dividing line between them is not precise. The role of established tourism enterprises in these two mechanisms may be quite small, but they can make a very significant contribution in fostering initiative and partnering the poor. These two mechanisms require significant efforts by the poor themselves, especially mechanism 4.

Mechanisms 5, 6 and 7 are very different from the first four mechanisms. Here, the poor are not necessarily active at all but rather are recipients of money or other support or wider benefits arising as a result of tourism. With Mechanisms 5 and 6, tourism enterprises or tourists can be the source of support in either case; the difference between them rests with whether the provision of support is voluntary or through some compulsory charge. Mechanism 7 is a more indirect process and may occur as an unplanned consequence of tourism related development or may occur by design.

Selecting different mechanisms

The choice of mechanisms to focus on will depend on the objectives and context of the situation. This relates back to the systematic analysis and assessment presented in part 1, which should inform the prioritisation and choice of actions and the selection of mechanisms. Much depends on the size and position of the private sector, the nature and location of the poor to be targeted and the scale of change sought. Some possible scenarios are illustrated in table 6.

The mechanisms are interrelated. It is also possible that one may lead on to another.

For example:

- An individual involved in informal selling (3) could be helped to establish a more formal micro enterprise (4).

- Voluntary giving of time and money by a well established private enterprise (6) could directly assist the establishment of a community-based enterprise (4).

- Poor households largely seeing their benefit from tourism coming indirectly through supplying a product to a tourism enterprise (2) may sell that same product directly to tourists (3); or vice versa – poor households who start with selling a product directly to tourists, may later sign a contract with a tourism enterprise to supply this product.

- Tourists charged an admission to a national park, with a percentage going to the poor (5), might be invited to top this up with additional voluntary giving (6).

- A tourism development project that invests in a new road to the village so helping the community (7) could contract local labour for its construction (2) and eventually retain them on its staff (1).

- Employees working in a tourism enterprise (1) could go on to use their training and experience to establish their own small business (4); or vice versa – local people who have gained experience in a small tourism enterprise, may obtain better paid employment in a large tourism enterprise.

Table 6   Scenarios for the use of different mechanisms

Situation	Particular mechanisms to consider
Sizeable presence of private sector tourism enterprises – hotels, catering etc. and a nearby large urban/rural poor.	Increasing the proportion of jobs filled by local poor (1) maybe the most sustainable mechanism but there may be limited new jobs available. High volumes of poor may be reachable through supply chains (2) and informal out of pocket spending by tourists (3). Voluntary giving could also help (6).
Relatively remote rural communities with few attractions and little current tourist visitation.	Location may restrict opportunities for direct engagement with tourists and feasible travel to work. Main potential may rest with supply chain (2), but poor could also benefit from general support from taxation revenue (5). In some situations private sector operators may invest in joint ventures (4).
Resort area with high visitation but few established tourism enterprises.	The main opportunity may rest with improving the management of the large amount of informal trading that is likely in such an area, increasing returns from this to the poor (3). Possibly some opportunities to establish some more formal businesses involving the poor (4). Voluntary giving could also help (6).
Poor communities in or near to attractive national park with some visitor throughput and a few established ecolodges.	Various mechanisms may present opportunities here, including establishing community-based initiatives or joint ventures (4), strengthening links with the existing ecolodges (1, 2, 6), and gaining benefit from national park entrance fees (5) or park related infrastructure (7).
Communities with little potential/capacity to engage directly or indirectly in tourism but with clear social deprivation and needs.	Many of the mechanisms could be ruled out here but tourism can still provide benefit to such communities, including schemes that reach the most needy poor, through taxation/charges (5) and more directly via voluntary giving (6) and possibly via collateral benefit such as infrastructure (7).
Area with expanding tourism sector including physical development projects, with a poor local population.	Opportunities may exist here to create the right conditions for new employment (1) and supply chain links (2) to the incoming enterprises, foster associated micro enterprises (4) and ensure collateral benefits to local residents (7).

NB: It is extremely important that these 7 mechanisms are not considered in isolation from each other. A destination may well set up projects or make functional interventions, such as capital investment or training programmes, that strengthen the chances of the poor to gain benefit through a number of the mechanisms. Likewise, the relationship between individual private sector operators and poor communities may be shaped through various of these mechanisms at any one time.

How part 2 is structured

The following sections look at each of these mechanisms in turn. In each case information is presented on:

- what the mechanism covers;

- the particular advantage of the mechanism;

- enabling conditions for the mechanism;

- challenges and issues with its implementation;

- actions to take at a destination level.

Actions can involve a number of stakeholders. Many should be seen as involving the public and private sectors working together and supported by NGOs. Therefore, the actions have been written primarily with a DM group in mind that can coordinate action on the ground.

Although sets of actions are presented under each of the seven mechanisms, some of the actions described will be relevant to more than one mechanism. The actions should therefore be considered together as well as separately.

 **Considering the range of mechanisms for reaching the poor**

1 Think about the range of mechanisms described here for channelling benefits from tourism to the poor.

 – Are you clear about the mechanisms and the differences between them?

 – For each mechanism, think of some of the situations where they may be applied.

2 Try to relate this presentation of mechanisms to the analysis of the situation in your area, as described in part 1. Which of these mechanisms do you feel offers most potential in your destination?

2.1 Employment of the Poor in Tourism Enterprises

This is about tourism enterprises providing jobs that are accessible to the poor and are of sufficient quality to raise them and their dependents above the poverty line. It is concerned with paid employment, rather than self-employment. It can involve all kinds of tourism enterprise, large and small, including hotels, restaurants, attractions, tour operators etc. which may be locally or internationally owned.

In many destinations that have been studied it has been found that direct employment has delivered the greatest contribution from tourism to poverty alleviation. While the actual proportion of tourism spending received by the employing company which reaches the poor may often be quite small, the gross impact is often high in volume terms.

Advantages of this mechanism

• It can potentially reach large numbers of poor people and their families.

• It directly links the poor with the mainstream of tourism.

• A good, permanent job can instil confidence and self respect, generating wider social benefits.

• Necessary entrepreneurial skills are provided by the employer.

• Some of the risk is borne by the employer.

• Pay is normally regular and reliable while employment lasts.

The tourism sector and individual enterprises can benefit from employing poor people from the local destination and offering them fair pay and conditions as it can:

• reduce staff turnover – local people close to their families often stay longer;

• result in high staff morale, which is reflected in the quality of service to guests;

• create greater local distinctiveness, appreciated by guests;

• strengthen relations with the local community, resulting in a more secure and positive environment for business.

> **Box 13 Employment data from accommodation enterprises**[2]
>
> In Madikwe Game Reserve, South Africa, a cluster of accommodation enterprises together provided jobs for 353 local employees in 2003. An analysis of economic flows from tourism revealed that formal employment constituted a dominant proportion of total economic benefits. For every local person in employment, benefits accrued to a further five dependents. Calculations of wage rates and employment totals have led to an estimate that tourism boosted average household income by 66% over 8 years up to 2007.
>
> The five year period from 2003 to 2007 saw a significant rise in employment in the tourism enterprises, with an even higher share of this going to local people (rising from 65% to 75%)
>
> In the commercial lodges local people earn 48% of the wage bill. This proportion has remained rather static in the five year period, reflecting the fact that there the rate of conversion of local people from unskilled to skilled employees has been low. A local skills deficiency identified in 2003 still persisted in 2007, suggesting that if destination developers are to maximise local socioeconomic benefit they must include training in their expenditure budgets.

Enabling conditions

- Established tourism enterprises regularly recruiting staff, and/or

- New enterprises being developed or planned which will require a labour force.

- Location of enterprises near to poor communities, with feasible travel to work.

- Enterprises pre-disposed and willing to employ the poor.

- Poor people prepared to work in tourism jobs.

Issues and challenges

- New jobs may not be available.

- The jobs available may not be well suited to the needs and skills of the poor.

- Benefits from employment may reach a few people rather than many.

- Pay and conditions in the tourism sector are sometimes exploitative.

- Opportunities for women and minorities can be limited.

- Poor people may not be well prepared for tourism employment.

An obvious challenge is simply the ability to provide new jobs within the tourism sector. In many destinations, this may require new investment and market growth. However, there appears to be quite a wide variation between different types of tourism enterprise and between individual enterprises in the relative proportion of poor people employed. This suggests that there may be reasonable scope to increase impacts on poverty over time through relating jobs better to the poor rather than just creating new ones.

A problem with direct employment as a mechanism for poverty alleviation is that it can be rather inflexible and not necessarily well suited to the poor. Jobs may exist in the wrong locations and at the wrong times.

---

2   Relly, 2008.

Often, there is willingness in principle among entrepreneurs to employ local people, yet they cannot afford to invest in their training and therefore end up recruiting educated people from town/richer families.

In some communities the provision of jobs in tourism for a few people can exacerbate economic differences and actually increase relative poverty levels for some people. A policy of spreading the benefits of tourism employment widely, to reach as many households as possible, can help to prevent this while also maximising the chances for poverty alleviation.

The quality of jobs in tourism is a major issue. The sector has been criticised for providing unstable and seasonal jobs, with poor pay and conditions and unsocial working hours.[3] Job security and rights, together with employee representation, are often limited. Remuneration levels in many tourism jobs are heavily dependent on gratuities, which may be unreliable and unfairly distributed.

In some countries, the proportion of tourism jobs held by women is very low, but a more widespread problem is a tendency for women's jobs in tourism to be seen as naturally falling in the lower end of the service provision – cleaning, food preparation etc. Few women are found in managerial positions.

Challenges and issues do not only relate to job supply. Barriers to employment in the sector include lack of awareness or poor image of tourism amongst poor communities, meaning that they do not even consider this as an employment option. Recruitment mechanisms can also be inaccessible to the poor. A significant problem is often the mismatch of skills possessed by the poor and those required to work in tourism, which may prevent them form being taken on by tourism enterprises or rising to higher positions.

Actions to pursue

► Shape jobs to the needs of the local poor

The level, size, duration and flexibility of jobs can affect the chances of them being taken up by the poor and maximising benefit to communities. In their human resource planning, enterprises should be encouraged and helped to look at local livelihood patterns, perhaps gaining advice from NGOs on this. If appropriate, employers should be encouraged to:

- Split up jobs into smaller parts. Job sharing could spread the benefits to more households.

- Enable multiple employment - providing part time employment which is regular and reliable and fits in with home caring, agriculture or other employment.

- Plan opportunities for poor people to enter at, or progress to, higher levels of jobs within a career path.

- Develop tourism products and activities based on local skills and knowledge. Examples include the use of local cuisine in restaurants and the provision of cultural tours that need local guides.

► Increase basic education levels and awareness of tourism

The likelihood of the poor being inclined or able to take up employment in tourism will depend partly on how prepared they are for this. Even quite basic jobs may require some level of educational attainment. Poor families, including young people in particular, should be given a picture of what jobs in tourism may be like, replacing images that may be too negative or rosy with real ones. Relevant actions include:

- Generally supporting local education. In the main, this lies outside the sphere of influence of tourism, but there are good examples of strong linkages between tourism enterprises and local schools – often as a form of self-interested philanthropy (see also mechanism 6).

---

3   Beddoe, 2004.

- Holding open days for local people to visit hotels etc.

- Offering short work experience placements or internships.

▶ Provide effective vocational training

The availability of appropriate training will increase the chances of poor people to meet standards required, gain more personal fulfilment and benefit from their work and progress to more senior positions. In many local destinations in developing countries, access to good quality training in hospitality, guiding and other tourism service and business skills is often very limited. This could be tackled at a destination level through a joint initiative between tourism enterprises (or their representative bodies) and local training institutions, supported by NGOs and with links to any national schemes. Elements should include:

- Being aware of employment opportunities in the area and structuring training to match with them, so ensuring that those trained have a good chance of moving into jobs. This should take account of the needs of existing employers and any new developments planned or proposed in the destination.

- Providing relevant, focused training courses that are accessible to the poor and actively promoted to them.

- Encouraging employers to provide on-the-job training and structure this to support career progression. Groups of enterprises could work together to prepare and deliver relevant short courses on specific skills.

- Making use of any incentives for training that may be provided nationally or more locally, such as tax offsetting or grant assistance.

- Helping local training providers and colleges to improve their resources and relevant skills. This should include ensuring adherence to standards, through verification and inspection. Supportive links between colleges/trainers and local enterprises should be encouraged.

Vocational training may help the poor not only to obtain direct employment in tourism enterprises but could also be relevant to their gaining benefit through mechanisms 2, 3 and 4.

Box 14 Training in advance of development[4]

Gran Pacifica is a major leisure and tourism development on the Pacific coast of Nicaragua. Hotels, condominiums, golf and sporting facilities and residential properties will come together in an extensive resort complex. In preparation for this, SNV has been working with people in the surrounding villages, providing capacity building relevant to the new jobs that will become available.

Initially, training focussed in the Villa del Carmen community. Vocational training has been provided in hospitality and other tourism related skills, languages, information technology, construction and carpentry. 390 people were trained in the first six months of the project, which spans a three year period. As well as training for direct employment, opportunities for engagement in the supply of produce and other services to the resort have also been addressed (mechanism 2).

The Gran Pacifica resort company is a partner in the initiative. The benefits to them include improved access to a local labour market, reduction in costs of services, and improved local business climate and image of the company.

▶ Open up and spread recruitment processes

The way that poor communities are made aware of new jobs that become available can affect the impact of employment benefit among the genuine poor. In order to increase the chances of reaching larger

---

4   From SNV Nicaragua.

numbers of dependents, jobs should ideally be spread between different families. This is more likely to happen through more open recruitment processes than by word of mouth from existing employees. Enterprises should be encouraged to:

- advertise jobs openly within communities;

- work with schools, local NGOs and others who can help to spread or target information to obtain maximum outreach.

▶ Address issues of physical accessibility

Local poor communities may not be able to benefit from new jobs created, simply because they have no means of travel to the workplace. Provision of sleeping quarters for staff can be a solution, but this has attendant problems of removing breadwinners from families and opening up jobs to in-migration. To tackle this:

- Consider accessibility to sources of labour supply amongst poor communities in future master planning for tourism in the destination, and when weighing up the merits of individual development proposals.

- Review transport provision between the main hotel/resort areas and poor communities (villages, suburbs). Enterprises could work together and with the public authorities to provide or subsidise buses for workers.

▶ Provide fair terms and conditions of employment

The poor are particularly vulnerable to exploitation by employers and to the consequences of loss of jobs and earnings. In recognition of this employers should:

- offer levels of pay that provide fair compensation for work undertaken while avoiding severe distortion of local pay structures;

- provide contracts for all employees, including those who are working part time;

- ensure good working conditions in terms of heath and safety, working hours and leave time;

- make provision for basic benefits and insurance cover relating to loss of earnings, redundancy and retirement;

- avoid over-dependency on service charges or gratuities in devising pay scales, while also ensuring equitable access to gratuities for all staff;

- ensure that seasonal workers are able to return, where possible, to the same job in subsequent seasons.

▶ Provide employment opportunities for women, minorities and selected priority groups

Tourism employment opportunities should be available for all without prejudice. However, to really make a difference in some destinations it may be necessary to be more proactive in the provision and promotion of specific opportunities for women and certain groups. This may require agreement to:

- avoid all prejudice (perceived or actual) against potential employees on the grounds of gender, age, and race;

- encourage applications from women for jobs at all levels;

- establish and support specific proactive initiatives aimed at providing employment opportunities for women, minorities and specific ethnic groups;

- establish and support programmes which provided starter jobs coupled with training for young people with particular needs.

Box 15 Creating opportunities for women in mountain trekking[5]

Trekking in Nepal is a male dominated activity. Two initiatives illustrate proactive approaches to provide opportunities for women.

In 1999 the **3 Sisters Trekking and Adventure Company** created the local NGO, Empowering Women of Nepal (EWN), with the objective of improving the lives of disadvantaged women through adventure tourism. Together they have combined practical skill-based training programmes with gainful employment opportunities, focusing on the trekking industry. Taking forward this initiative has been a challenge due to social prejudices. Nevertheless, over a five year period 3 Sisters trained more than 300 women between 16 to 30 years old from 33 districts of Nepal. The training sessions were free of costs and are largely funded by the revenues of the trekking company and from donations. The programme provided the supportive environment that the women need to build the necessary confidence to become successful tourism professionals. Income received by female porters and guides is in line with that paid to males.

As part of the *MAST* project (see box 11, p53) **Himalayan Encounters,** a medium-sized trekking and white water rafting company, adopted a gender diversity employment initiative and committed themselves to hiring female staff. In April 2007 it advertised job positions in the local communities where it operates and hired eight women. The company also provided on-the-job training to each of the new staff members to increase their skills in the hospitality/tourism sector. The initiative increased the quality of services to women clients, as they now provide female guides to those who prefer them, as well as having positive social impacts. It created economic independence among women who were previously dependent on their male counterparts. In 2008 it was estimated that each female staff member of the company earned 35 Euros and the trekking guides earned 25 Euros per month.

One of the important lessons learned from the initiative is that the companies promoting gender diversity by hiring more female staff should also provide gender sensitivity training to all staff members, which could largely prevent sexual harassments.

▶ **Seek to strengthen employment legislation, including minimum wage requirements, and adherence to it**

It has been demonstrated that the presence of a minimum wage can significantly improve the proportion of tourism earnings that accrue to the poor. While destinations may only be able to press for this, together with any other legislative backing to the actions outlined above, they should actively work to ensure compliance in their area. This will require good collaboration between stakeholders.

▶ **Recognise and encourage employee empowerment**

There are a number of examples where greater awareness of rights and responsibilities by employees and employers has led to increased benefits on both sides and improved quality for visitors. By acting together individuals can make sure that their position and needs are better understood. This should involve:

- Advocacy and awareness-raising on the rights of employees, based on international norms and/or national legislation, concerning wage levels, conditions, safety, discrimination etc.

- Encouraging and respecting unionisation of labour and establishment of specific associations to represent the interests of employees in particular jobs and negotiate on their behalf.

---

5   From: SNV Nepal, 2006 and United Nations Environment Programme, 2008.

2.1 Considering the employment mechanism

1 Based on your analysis of current and future tourism in the destination:

  – Do you believe there are opportunities for existing enterprises to provide more direct employment for the poor?

  – Are there new developments proposed or planned which will be seeking to recruit employees?

2 What are the main barriers preventing the recruitment of the poor to tourism jobs? Are general education levels and awareness/image of tourism issues? Or is it more about a mismatch of skills or physical accessibility?

3 Think about the provision for vocational training in tourism in the destination. Does it exist – could it be improved? Is it truly accessible to the poor? Are private sector enterprises involved? How can employers and trainers be best brought together?

4 Consider what you know about the terms and conditions of employees in the tourisms sector in the destination. Is it possible that they may be too low, so that employees remain in poverty? Are labour regulations in place and enforced and employees rights upheld?

5 Have you previously identified gender, youth and minority groups as targets for poverty alleviation? If so, are jobs and training fully accessible to them?

2.2 Supply of Goods and Services to Tourism Enterprises

This is about improving the livelihoods of the poor through strengthening their engagement in the provision of goods and services to tourism enterprises in the destination. Here, the poor are suppliers, sometimes under contact, but are not employees. This is an indirect process of linking the poor to tourism spending, based on strengthening local supply chains. In the main, this mechanism does not involve any contact between the poor and tourists, although some contracted services may be delivered directly to tourists.

Goods and services may be supplied during the development phase – for example, in the provision of materials and labour for construction – or as an input to the operation of a tourism enterprise.

Typically, goods and services provided through local supply chains may include:

• food and drink for hotels and restaurants to use in their kitchens or to sell directly to tourists;

• soft furnishings, utensils and other consumable items (e.g. decorative artworks, tablemats, cosmetics, staff uniforms etc.);

• maintenance work, gardening, laundry services supplied under contract;

• supply of items to be retailed to tourists by the enterprise (e.g. handicrafts);

• provision of excursions to tourists under contract and sold through the hotel/resort (e.g. transport services, guiding etc.);

• provision of various additional experiences (e.g. hairdressing, massage, cultural entertainment) offered and sold through the enterprise.

Within local tourism supply chains, the provision of agricultural produce stands out as an activity of immense importance in delivering income benefits to poor communities, owing to the sheer volume and value of food purchasing as an input to the tourism sector[6] and the significant importance of agriculture as a source of livelihood for many poor people.

Partly for this reason, it has been found that this mechanism often accounts for a very significant proportion of pro-poor income from tourism in many destinations in developing countries.[7]

Advantages of this mechanism

- It can provide an additional source of income for many poor households.

- It can bring benefit from tourism to more remote communities unlikely to be visited by tourists.

- It mainly does not require beneficiaries to have tourism related skills or to interact with tourists.

- It makes use of and further develops traditional skills and resources of local people and complements traditional livelihoods.

- It can reach the genuine poor.

- It can lead to stable, supportive relationships with private enterprises.

This mechanism also brings advantages to the tourism enterprises themselves through:

- enabling them to offer fresh produce, which is tastier, healthier and more likely to be organic;

- strengthening their local distinctiveness;

- potentially reducing costs – for example in transport;

- providing a selling point and good public relations with existing and potential new customers;

- adding to staff interest and morale;

- securing support from local communities with whom they may otherwise have little contact.

Enabling conditions

- The presence of tourism enterprises (hotels etc.) in the area seeking supplies;

- willingness by these enterprises to audit their supplies and to procure from the poor;

- local climatic and soil conditions suited to growing or rearing appropriate foodstuffs;

- farming structures involving engagement of the poor;

- ability/skills of the poor in producing other materials;

- support services to assist development, linkages and coordination;

- practicable feasibility of transporting produce from suppliers to enterprises.

---

6   In Mexico, spending on food in restaurants, cafes, shops etc. accounts for one third of all tourist expenditure (Torres and Momsen, 2004). In Luang Prabang, Laos, over half of the US$ 6 million p.a. earned by the poor comes from the supply of food and drink – directly and via the supply chain. (Ashley, 2006b).

7   In some destinations the poor earn between one third and a half of their aggregate tourism income through supply chains rather than directly (Ashley and Haysom, 2008).

Issues and challenges

- Tourism enterprises may need not be concerned about their sources of supply.

- They may be reluctant to provide the time necessary to investigate options.

- They may have doubts about the ability of poor suppliers to provide the quality and dependability needed.

- Poor suppliers may find it hard to meet the requirements of tourism enterprises.

- Distribution systems may prove to be difficult or costly.

Sourcing new suppliers and then making changes can be a time consuming and costly activity for tourism enterprises. Their attitude to this will partly be dictated by their owners' and managers' overall attitude to community relations and poverty alleviation in the context of corporate social responsibility. Positive personal commitment will be important. However, enterprises will also need to see clear benefits for their business.

Evidence on business attitudes suggests that in principle many would seek to favour local suppliers. Market research in The Gambia showed that over 75% of hotels, shops and restaurants would prefer to buy directly from local growers if quality of supply could be assured.[8] The problem is scepticism over the latter condition. Chefs, who have most say over food sourcing, often doubt the ability of local farmers to meet their high standards. Other standards, especially relating to food hygiene, may be imposed on the enterprises by national or international regulations or by the requirements of tour operators using the enterprise. In addition to quality, reliability of supply over a specified season and capacity to meet the volumes required are major issues. At the end of the day it can be easier for chefs to deal with a few established wholesalers.

The concerns of enterprises are often justified. Poor suppliers face many difficulties in meeting procurement requirements. These may include lack of skills and resources, financial insecurity and problems with access and communications. In agriculture, local growing conditions may pose limitations. However, many of these problems can be overcome with assistance.

By providing a sizeable market, tourism enterprises can deliver significant benefits to suppliers of food and other goods and services in poor communities. However, it is important to guard against potential negative impacts on communities. For example, demands from tourism can distort local markets, leading to price rises and shortages of supply, resulting in greater overall relative poverty. This requires careful planning, involving people who understand the basis of rural livelihoods and traditional agriculture.

Where destinations have undertaken a value chain analysis (see section 1.4) this may have lead to greater awareness of supply chains generally in the destination.

In order to develop this mechanism, however, individual enterprises should be encouraged to make a detailed audit of their suppliers and to take action. Much can be gained by coordinating this locally.

Fundamentally, the challenge and the opportunity is for tourism enterprises and potential local suppliers to be helped to come together and to understand each other better.

Actions to pursue

▶ Plan supply chain optimisation as an integral part of future destination development

The clear importance of retaining income and providing opportunities for the poor through local supply chains means that this process should be given highest priority by destinations. While successful initiatives have been taken by some locations and especially by certain individual hotels, it is often a

---

8   Pro Poor Tourism Pilots, 2004.

hard, time consuming, costly and slow process to change established practices. Therefore destinations should:

- Work with investors and local communities at the earliest planning stage of new developments to set up linkages before supply chains are built.

- Promote the use of locally supplied materials and labour at the construction stages of new development. If possible, this should be made a requirement of permissions to develop – through the granting of concessions, licences or planning permission.

▶ Encourage and help tourism enterprises to audit their suppliers

It is hard to make improvements, both broadly within the destination and individually by separate enterprises, without a clear understanding of current sources of supply. Enterprises, particularly at senior management level, may be not be aware of all their sources and may well know little about the circumstances of their suppliers and their own supply chains – i.e. the degree to which they are already pro-poor. The process of auditing can be quite time consuming. This could be made easier with some guidance and coordination at a destination level, including:

- Providing questionnaires which enterprises can use and suggesting tips for approaching suppliers. Questions should cover: employees, employment policy and practice, environmental policy and practice, and their own procurement policy. Supply issues and future opportunities might also be covered.

- Coordinating approaches to certain suppliers who may be used by a number of enterprises, and sharing responses from them, so they are not approached repeatedly.

- Providing some incentives for engagement in the exercise.

Following the audit, enterprises should list their products that are currently sourced from non-local suppliers or those which do not benefit the poor. They should then consider which of these might be possibly be sourced differently.

Box 16 Spier – comprehensive supplier assessment[9]

In 2004, Spier Leisure embarked on a systematic review of its procurement practice, starting with its 155-bed hotel with conference centre just outside Stellenbosch in South Africa. The review was part of a wider shift towards the integration of a pro-poor agenda at a strategic level within the whole organization. Spier set out to measure its current supply chain performance, to set new priorities and to select performance indicators which would measure its success.

A questionnaire was sent to all Spier Leisure suppliers, with 60 questions grouped into nine areas including traditional procurement questions such as quality alongside less traditional questions about treatment of staff or the degree of black ownership. It was essential to understand the starting point if Spier's new procurement policy was to be effective in prioritising suppliers that were local, small and black-owned. An input tool was developed and a scoring system devised which could be visually represented on a spider diagram. It was found that the actual processes of contacting suppliers created interest amongst them in the issues covered.

After the first batch of replies were received, the system was discussed and refined before being rolled out across the supply chains in relation to the whole of Spier's business. At this stage, over 550 questionnaires were returned, representing over 80% of suppliers. Spier learned that many of their suppliers were already small companies, but not necessarily local and only one in eight were 'black economically empowered' (BEE) suppliers. It was clear that there was work to be done, as Spier's suppliers were performing well below their own record measured against the same criteria.

---

9   Ashley and Haysom, 2008 and 2009.

Rigorous criteria and targets were set for shifting procurement, and new processes put in place to evaluate every new supplier. As a result, over four years the percentage of procurement spend going to local suppliers more than doubled, as did the percentage of suppliers that are BEE.

Spier subsequently assisted its supplier base to make changes. Input involved mentoring, innovative financing and the establishment of an enterprise development programme to develop new black local suppliers.

▶ Investigate and disseminate information on suppliers in the destination

Identifying new suppliers and finding out about them and their pro-poor credentials can also be a time consuming process. A coordinated approach in the destination could be of great assistance here in providing information on local suppliers of a range of produce and services. This could involve:

- compiling a database of suppliers, built up over time through various means, including observation and word of mouth;

- gathering and maintaining information from them;

- making this information available to tourism enterprises on request – through published lists etc.;

- holding events at which suppliers can meet enterprises.

Intermediaries, such as wholesalers who may be locally based, can play a very important role in the process and make it more efficient. They should be encouraged to adopt pro-poor principles in their work, in their own sourcing and dealings with producers and in the information they provide on the products they handle.

▶ Promote and encourage good practice in procurer-supplier relationships

The nature of the relationship established between individual tourism enterprises and their supplier is critical to ongoing success and to ensuring that benefits are delivered that meet the needs of the poor. This is really a matter for the enterprises themselves, but DM groups may be in a position to provide some guidance and facilitate sharing of experience. Lessons recorded from existing successful projects point to a number of key elements, including:

- providing clear simple contacts, so everyone knows what is expected;

- ensuring that the supplier is able to deliver – this may be helped by splitting the contract into separate components;

- appointing someone from the enterprise's staff to promote and manage local supplier contacts – but also engaging all staff in this so they can foster the relationship;

- paying promptly, if possible immediately on supply.

Some enterprises have found it necessary, and valuable, to provide a lot of support early on to their suppliers. This has included advice, specific technical assistance and ongoing mentoring, especially to help the supplier reach the quality of product or service required, and sometimes financial support. Some suppliers who may have been trading informally may have been helped by the enterprise to set up their own more formal business. This could include the establishment of a joint venture between the enterprise and the supplier.

▶ Raise the profile of the tourism-agriculture/fisheries link

The opportunities for mutual support between these important economic sectors, and the range of players and support services involved, suggests that integration should not be left simply to individual initiative. Profile raising can occur at two levels:

- Agreeing a clear policy in the destination to strengthen the link, committing public sector agencies, agricultural support services (and fisheries where relevant), NGOs and other stakeholders to action.

- Establishing a communication campaign to strengthen awareness of local produce, amongst local stakeholders and also amongst tourists. This could involve some kind of produce branding.

Box 17 A comprehensive campaign, Jamaica[10]

The 'Eat Jamaican' campaign was launched in 2003 by several Jamaican associations including the Jamaica Agricultural Society (JAS), to promote locally-produced goods to residents, visitors and exporters. The campaign saw SuperClubs, one of the leading all-inclusive tourism companies globally, making commitments to support the produce of local farmers. In 2004, SuperClubs signed a Memorandum of Understanding with JAS. Under the MOU, SuperClubs agreed to trade with the JAS through a Central Marketing Company, to work with the JAS to provide incentives for local farmers and to assist with designing technical assistance programmes for JAS members. In addition to providing good PR and marketing, sourcing high quality local fruit and vegetables was a key reason for SuperClubs' involvement.

▶ Consider establishing a tourism and agriculture/fisheries support project

There are many good examples round the world of close relationships being established between individual hotels (including resorts and lodges) and local farmers from neighbouring poor communities. Often, this is at the instigation of the hotel. In can involve strong relationships forming between chefs and farmers so each becomes aware of the others' needs and capabilities. A number of hotels have helped farmers introduce new crops, supplying know-how, seeds and other necessary investments to secure successful production. Individual initiatives and relationships of this kind should be encouraged.

The very fragmented nature of agricultural production, fisheries and sometimes tourism in many destinations, however, often points to the advantage of establishing coordinated projects, bringing together a number of farmers or fishermen who are then helped to supply to clusters of hotels and restaurants. Tourism enterprises could also be encouraged to work with each other on developing supply chains as sometimes individual businesses cannot justify the effort and investment needed in communicating with supplies and helping them. Economies of scale, both for procurers and suppliers can make returns on the effort needed more worthwhile. A DM group could provide leadership for such projects, in conjunction with NGOs.

Past experience suggests that particular attention should be paid to:

- Building trust with the suppliers. This is critical to success – some projects have folded because suppliers felt they were being treated unfairly.

- Providing the right facilitators. Mistrust often centres on 'middlemen'. Facilitators must have technical competence and relate well to their clients on both sides.

- Taking well paced steps. Small, relatively quick wins build confidence.

- Choosing crops carefully. A number of studies have shown that certain types of crops, such as higher priced vegetables and fruits, can deliver better returns.[11] There is also an advantage in concentrating on crops that are locally distinctive, such as seafood.

- Assisting with appropriate technology. Joint initiatives can help justify investment in special solutions to overcome soil, climate and seasonality challenges, such as provision of glasshouses or hydroponics and storage.

---

10   Pro Poor Tourism Pilots, 2004.

11   In St Lucia an initiative by Sandals resorts to source watermelons locally delivered an income of US$ 100/month for 70 families, bring them above the poverty line.

- Practical training and demonstration. Most projects underline the importance of learning by observing and doing.

- Inviting farmers to visit hotels/restaurants to see how their produce is used.

- Logistics of distribution. Collecting produce from remote producers and distributing it to users is often a sizeable challenge.

Box 18 Examples of agriculture-tourism support projects

Mexico – Problems with middlemen[12]

The resort of Cancun receives over 3m visitors a year, one quarter of all Mexico's tourists. In 1988, an early government scheme supported producers in the state of Quintana Roo to supply hotels in Cancun with fresh produce such as papaya. The government identified the buyers and markets, and provided transport. Some farmers dropped out over time, disagreeing with the terms and prices on offer, but others carried on, restructuring their production to create a year round supply. Further withdrawals occurred, due to mistrust of the middlemen and government officials and eventually the scheme stopped. However, in a new initiative, the Mayor of Cancun invited producers to participate in a fruit exhibition in the Cancun hotel zone. This has led to at least one of the original farmers from the government scheme selling direct to hotels. The Oasis Hotel, the largest in Cancun, sends a truck directly to Laguna Berrero to buy papayas, oranges, lemons and watermelons from local farmers.

Bwindi, Uganda[13]

The Bwindi Impenetrable Forest National Park attracts thousands of tourists every year but local communities gain little from their presence. For this reason the Bwindi Advanced Market Gardener's Association (AMGARA) was established to create opportunities for local farmers to produce foods to supply to the tourism industry, involving the training of farmers, the bulking and grading of produce and marketing it to the tour camps. Started in 2007 with NGO support, AMGARA had 120 member households in 2009. Members pay a joining fee and annual subscription and elect an Executive Committee. A central feature is the project's demonstration garden. Training, which includes various agricultural techniques including intermediate technologies and business skills, has been a key part of the benefit provided. The families involved have also gained nutritional benefit. Lack of transport has proved a considerable challenge however, as members have had to bring in the crops themselves which has proved very hard for more remote farmers.

▶ **Strengthen the supply of services, including complementary visitor experiences, by the poor to tourism enterprises**

Although some of the above actions may focus on the supply of goods and produce, especially food, it is important to stress that the actions should also apply to a range of services as well, including those listed at the beginning of this section. Such services should equally be subject to auditing, linkage building etc. as described above.

This should include the provision of certain services that may actually be provided directly to tourists, but sold and promoted through the main enterprise. The latter may be a hotel, for example, which may offer an excursion to tourists either as part of its own range of services or as something which it endorses or with which it is associated. The poor can benefit considerably from such an arrangement, which provides an access to market for them as well as possible advice and support from the enterprise. The enterprise, in turn, sees benefit either simply from enhancing its appeal to guests or possibly from a financial arrangement with the poor supplier, such as a small commission.

---

12   Torres and Momsen, 2004.

13   Sandbrook, 2009.

▶ Maximise opportunities for retailing through tourism enterprises

Established tourism enterprises often include retail outlets from which tourists can buy. A typical example is a souvenir shop or kiosk in the foyer of a hotel. The stocking of such outlets can be seen as part of the supply chain of the enterprise and should also be the subject of careful auditing and action to increase linkages with poor suppliers. Some enterprises make arrangements for poor producers to retail (and possibly demonstrate) their products themselves within their property – this essentially overlaps with mechanism 3 (see later).

▶ Help to remove barriers for the poor in engaging in the supply chain

In each destination there may be a number of local issues that make it difficult for poor communities, individuals and families to engage in the supply chain. Some of these may be similar to those for small and micro businesses in general, which are covered under mechanism 4. The actions listed under that mechanism are relevant to the process of working with communities to develop enterprises that feed in to the supply chain. Particular issues that have arisen elsewhere in relation to the supply chain, and which could be addressed within the destination include:

- Helping suppliers obtain access to credit. The existence of an established contact with tourism enterprises should be able to be taken into account.

- Providing general business training and support.

2.2 Considering the supply chain mechanism

1 Think about all the types of goods and services that are supplied to tourism enterprises. Consider what you know about these supply chains already in your destination – which may have been informed by the kind of analysis outlined in part 1.

2 To gain more benefit for the poor, tourism enterprises need to know a lot about a) their current sources of supply and b) what it available locally, especially from poor communities. How do you think they could be encouraged and helped in this within your destination? Can you help with the flow of information, for example?

3 Think about the links between tourism and agriculture/fisheries in your destination.

   – Do the people involved, both at a policy level and practically, work together? How could this be strengthened?

   – Is there a possibility of establishing a specific project to strengthen links between local farmers and tourism enterprises?

4 Are there particular barriers that appear to be preventing poor communities participating in the supply of goods and services to tourism enterprises – could these be overcome?

5 How possible do you think it would be to take supply chain issues into account when planning future tourism development in the destination?

2.3 Informal Selling of Goods and Services to Tourists by the Poor

This is about the selling of goods and services directly to tourists by the poor. They will mainly be individual traders, largely unregulated – part of the informal economy.

Typical examples include general street sellers, handicraft producers and sellers, informal guides and porters, entertainers, people offering motorised and non-motorised transport, simple food and drink dispensers and providers of basic unlicensed accommodation.

Informal sellers of this kind are found in almost all developing countries and are often numerous. They are important recipients of the significant levels of casual out-of-pocket spending incurred by tourists and the vast majority are poor.

This mechanism is principally about managing informal selling and improving the benefits to those involved. The process of management and improvement may lead to participants establishing or combining into more formal enterprises, which would then become subject to the support outlined in mechanism 4.

Advantages of this mechanism

- It can reach large numbers of poor individuals directly.

- It accounts for a sizeable proportion of tourists' spending. For example, the informal economy accounts for around one third of daily expenditure of tourists in the Gambia.[14]

- Recipients are more likely to be genuine poor than those engaged in formal tourism employment or enterprises.

- The activity is readily easily accessed, by both men and women.

- It can support certain types of trading that is also providing a service to local people.

- In certain circumstances informal trading can provide part of the colour and atmosphere of destinations sought out by tourists.

Enabling conditions

- A good flow of tourists exists in the destination.

- They have enough time to make local purchases and are encouraged to do so by tour operators.

- Poor people in the area are capable of producing and/or selling products which are relevant and attractive to tourists.

- Sellers are prepared to improve standards, including working together to do so.

Issues and challenges

- Sellers may not understand tourists and their needs and interests.

- Tourists may be inhibited from buying from street sellers.

- Chaotic selling conditions and competition reduce potential benefits.

- Sellers may resist making improvements or working together.

- Regulations and raising standards may place barriers in the way of the more needy poor.

- Informal sellers are in conflict with the formal tourism sector.

While many of the goods and services sold are well received by tourists and the interaction with local people is valued, low and often inconsistent quality remains a challenge. A lack of market understanding, leading to a mismatch between goods on sale and what tourists are looking for, can reduce the amount sold and incomes earned by the poor. Tourists may be inhibited from buying owing to concerns about hygiene (relating to food purchases) or safety (relating to guiding and transport) which may sometimes be well founded.

14   Bah and Goodwin, 2003.

Informal selling is often characterised by extreme competition and over supply. This serves to drive down prices. The process can also be very inefficient, with traders spending a great deal of time in making very few sales. It is also widely open to misuse of child labour. Exploitation of buyers and sellers is a further problem, with bartering being seen by tourists as common practice, sometimes leading to unpleasantness or transactions that are unfair to the seller. The chaotic nature of informal selling, frequently involving hassling of tourists, can be counterproductive.

Change is difficult to bring about. Informal traders can be reluctant to abide by codes and rules. However, a number of projects have demonstrated what can be achieved by sellers working together and making simple agreements.

A fundamental conundrum is that organization and regulation of the process can lead to improved quality and efficiency, with better returns to those involved, but can raise barriers which deny opportunities to others, reducing the potential for more poor people to gain a little benefit from tourist spending. In certain circumstances formalisation may also reduce the appeal to visitors. It is therefore important to strike a balance and pay careful attention to the detail in any regulations that are made, being aware of the consequences for all involved.

The relationship between informal traders and formal tourism enterprises, large or small, can be tense. This may be as a result of competition between them for tourist spending – for example, informal guiding is seen as taking an important source of income away from tour operators or licensed guides. Another cause of tension relates to guests being disturbed by street or beach traders. The solution may be to encourage the informal sector to concentrate on activities that are complementary to formal sector enterprises rather an in competition with them.[15] An example would be the poor offering informal guided walks rather than competing to deliver complete excursions. One approach is to strengthen opportunities for the poor to sell goods and services to tourists through the formal sector, as in mechanism 2.

Actions to pursue

▶ Audit and monitor informal direct selling to tourists in the destination

Without gaining some objective understanding of the amount and nature of informal selling at the outset, it is difficult to assess the need and opportunity for any improvement. An indication of the overall importance of this activity in channelling tourist spending to the poor may have been obtained from the kinds of analysis outlined in section 1.4, including a visitor survey. However, more detail may be helpful. It is difficult and probably impossible to audit all activity, but an objective picture could be built up through:

- observing activity at different times of the year and day;

- talking to a sample of different kinds of traders;

- discussing this activity with local stakeholders to obtain feedback on issues, problems and ideas.

▶ Plan and create locations for direct selling

The location of sellers' pitches or stalls, or simply where they congregate can significantly affect both their success and any negative impacts they may have on tourists and formal enterprises. Ideally they should be well located with respect to visitor flows but not in places where they can cause bottlenecks or detract from the destination's main amenities. There may be no problem in the destination, but some actions to consider include:

- positive provision of specific well situated areas where trading is encouraged;

- introducing bylaws to restrict trading in certain areas;

---

15   Bah and Goodwin, 2003.

- providing facilities for traders to use, including stalls available at low rent;

- working with existing markets [16], which may be traditional and are often a key attraction to tourists, to see if they can be improved or better promoted, without destroying the atmosphere;

- developing and promoting new markets or handicraft centres as visitor attractions (these may possibly be specially themed to attract interest, but there are also advantages in having different types of trader side by side).

The provision of new markets has proved successful in a number of places. They should:

- have some pitches and basic stalls at sufficiently low rentals to attract the genuine poor. Short period rentals should be made available;

- be managed to create the right atmosphere for buying – avoiding excessive hassling and haggling but encouraging life, action, local colour;

- be open at the right times to attract visitors;

- be well promoted and included on all tourist circuits;

- enable traders to work together, stimulate and innovate, share transport to the market, etc.

Box 19 Luang Prabang Night Market[17]

The successful Luang Prabang Night Market in Lao PDR was started in 2002/03 and is open every day from dusk until about 10pm, with traditional craft producers selling an extensive collection of handicrafts such as textiles, clothing, carvings, and basketry. The range and variety of crafts in one place strengthens the appeal to visitors and the chances of stimulating impulse purchases. Low cost stalls are available, including for short periods which are of special value to village women making the return journey. They are thus accessible to producers without capital. By selling in one place, traders have learnt from each other and are able to share certain costs.

The market has become very popular, and established its reputation as a good experience and part of the tourist circuit. Therefore, both the volume and proportion of tourist spending on crafts has increased. Not only have existing producers earned more, sometimes through raising the quality of their product and its design, but some have also started to employ other people in their production. There has also been room for new producers to enter the market. One very important way of increasing pro-poor income is not necessarily visible to tourists at the market itself but relates to increasing the share of textiles using silk that comes from farmers in Lao PDR.

▶ Help sellers group and organise together

Much can be gained from traders working together. This enables them to:

- agree codes and rules, monitor adherence and confront abusers;

- lobby and represent the interests of the group;

- promote and raise the profile of the group's activities and seek linkages with others;

- agree on prices and avoid damaging competition;

- work together to improve standards;

- organise training, support and finance for the group and members.

---

16   In this section the word 'market' is used in this physical sense, i.e. a collection of stalls.

17   Ashley, 2006.

Action at a destination level could involve:

- Encouraging and facilitating the formation of general local traders associations, or different associations for the various specific types of trade or activity. The latter may be more effective as they can address common issues in detail. Sometimes it may be appropriate for trading associations to form around existing social groupings, such as women's groups.

- Helping with constitutions, advising on administrative arrangements, providing start up finance and helping to organise training.

- Seeking to ensure that the group remains open and does not prevent others joining.

- Supporting promotion and communication with other stakeholders, and linkages to national associations.

- Working with the group to agree on local standards and codes of practice

- Addressing issues raised by the group.

Box 20 Lumbini Rickshaw Pullers[18]

Lumbini, the birthplace of Lord Budda, is an important tourist destination in Nepal. Numerous rickshaw pullers in the area were competing openly with no organization and great inefficiency. Supported by the Tourism for Rural Poverty Alleviation Programme (TRPAP) and the Lumbini Development Trust (LDT), the Rickshaw Pullers Functional Group was established, with a membership of 70 pullers. The group has worked with LDT and others on a larger number of small practical issues, including the introduction of an officially recognised ID card, simple uniforms for members, setting and publicising reasonable prices, introducing a queuing system, introducing penalties against rule breakers, successfully lobbying for the restriction of four wheeled entry to the central area, making capital available to decorate and repair their rickshaws, and basic training in customer relations and English language. Agreed rules are monitored by TRPAP and LDT. The various improvements, together with promoting the destination and the use of local transport services, have led to an increase in earnings of the rickshaw pullers by 70%.

▶ Support appropriate regulation, licensing and formal recognition

Irrespective of whether groups/associations have been formed, attention should be paid to the status and rules of operation of trading in general in the destination, which may affect and assist individual traders. Issues to address are:

- The opportunity for certain traders to be formally recognised within national schemes or legislation, for example in registers and lists of guides, accommodation etc. This could help their position and enable them to obtain more support, including credit.

- Introduction of local regulations and codes which may in turn lead to some form of local recognition and labelling for those that comply.

- The auditing of legislation for language or regulations that may unnecessarily inhibit activity by the poor.

▶ Provide or support practical training, advice and assistance

Associations or individual traders should have access to support and assistance. The needs of local traders should be discussed with them to ensure that this is relevant to them and that they will respond. NGOs, training/ educational bodies and other relevant stakeholders should consider setting up short courses or direct advice surgeries which cover:

---

18   SNV Nepal, 2006.

- simple business processes, including pricing;

- selling and how to relate to tourists;

- product issues – sales items, design, quality, content of the service;

- presentation – improving appearance;

- hygiene and safety.

Consideration should also be given to strengthening access to credit through micro-finance agencies in the area (see mechanism 4).

▶ Encourage tourism enterprises to support local traders

This relates to the issue of tensions and potential for complementary activity between the formal sector and informal traders, raised above. Individual enterprises should be encouraged to form their own direct relationships with informal traders, but collective approaches can help with certain issues. Activity should include:

- Working out common positions on which kinds of services should be provided by the formal sector as against the informal sector – to reduce tension and competition.

- Encouraging hotels to provide sales outlets in their establishments or to invite traders to their premises at certain times (see mechanism 2).

- Encouraging hotels and tour operators to direct their guests to informal traders for certain services, help those traders devise products that are appropriate for their guests, and provide feedback to them.

- Discussing and seeking input to solutions relating to the physical management and location of traders.

Box 21 Cooperation with vendors in Phuket[19]

Laguna Phuket is an integrated resort in Thailand, where five hotels share a common infrastructure and facilities. The resort supported a community of informal vendors, mostly women selling an assortment of goods and services from wooden stalls. The beachfront hotels were protected by a headland from the full force of the Indian Ocean tsunami in December 2004, but the informal economy was devastated as the vendor stalls operating on the beach were washed away. However, the small traders proved quite resilient in the period following the tsunami. Two of the hotel managers in particular were willing to work with vendors, co-operating in the construction of new stalls and agreeing a revised layout. This met the twin goals of offering aid to individuals while raising the standards of service offered to visitors. In 2006 there were 50% more vendors than in 2004.

▶ Provide information to tourists about buying from local traders

It is important to bring tourist themselves into the picture. Some of the problems and missed opportunities for benefitting the poor through direct selling relate to uncertainty and lack of information and confidence amongst tourists. This could partly be addressed through:

- encouraging tour operators and local enterprises to inform their guests positively about how to relate to local traders, things to avoid, prices to expect, fair bartering processes etc.;

- providing information about these issues in print, local information centres etc. alongside promotion of the purchasing opportunities available.

---

19 Smith and Henderson, 2008.

▶ Address particular opportunities associated with handicrafts

The production and retailing of handicrafts to tourists as souvenirs is an important activity in most destinations in developing countries and is often carried on in the informal sector. Most of the actions outlined above are relevant to this.

Looking in more detail at the opportunities presented by handicrafts, some practical points on boosting sales are provided in Annex 3-B. Particular actions to pursue at a destination level include:

- Researching materials and designs that are locally distinctive and relate to local culture and traditions.

- Encouraging and helping craft makers to source their materials from poor suppliers. The sourcing of materials used by craft makers can have a significant effect on spreading the benefits more widely.[20]

- Advising on designs and types of product appropriate to different tourist market segments.

- Establishing a local brand/label for crafts made in the area which are meeting certain quality standards.

- Encouraging creativity and product differentiation so that people are not all selling the same thing.

- Facilitating opportunities for handicraft producers to demonstrate their skills.

▶ Pay particular attention to informal service provision

Provision of various services to tourists by the informal sector occurs in almost all destinations. Again, the actions set out in this section are relevant. However, particular attention should be addressed to three types of service which have their own particular issues and needs.

- Guiding. This is often seen as an easy-entry activity by the poor and especially young people. It can be helpful to establish a category of 'local guide' who is recognised, provided with some training, abides by simple codes, and works in with more formal qualified guides and tour operators.

- Catering. A primary concern of tourists is cleanliness and hygiene. Action at a destination level could include basic inspection of premises, advice on minimum standards, labelling and listing.

- Informal accommodation. This may include letting of rooms, bed and breakfast, or camping sites. It can be a difficult area to get this right. Issues for tourists include sanitation, communication and security. As with catering, local action should include inspection, advice and labelling. In certain markets it may work best if it is promoted and packaged as a genuine opportunity to experience local hospitality, in the form of homestays. This may be best if attached to national homestay programmes.

2.3 Considering the informal selling mechanism

1 Think about the amount of informal trading with tourists (including international and domestic markets) in the destinations. How much do you know about this? How could you find out more?

2 Are there particular problems associated with this activity – e.g. excessive competition, hassling etc. Does it need better management? Could the poor benefit more from it?

3 Are there locations that could be developed and managed better for informal trading - for example existing or new markets (bazaars)?

---

20   Ashley, 2006.

4 How well to the traders work together – is there scope for more local groups and organizations?

5 Is there any activity at the moment to provide informal traders with advice and assistance? Could this be provided? Are relevant regulations helpful – and are they applied?

6 What information are tourists given about purchasing from the informal sector, if any? Could there be better links between the informal and formal sectors?

7 Are there particular issues or opportunities in the destination concerning specific informal sectors, such as handicrafts, guiding and provision of accommodation and catering? Are these opportunities being maximised?

2.4 Developing Small/Micro or Community-based Tourism Enterprises or Joint Ventures

This action is about working with poor communities and individuals to develop or strengthen tourism enterprises.

This mechanism is different from mechanism 3 in that the latter is much more about management of informal trading that is likely to be happening anyway and seeking to gain more benefit from it. This mechanism 4 concentrates on development and growth - on working with poor communities or individuals on the establishment of sustainable tourism enterprises. In some situations this may involve a transition from an informal trading situation, which simply delivers income for immediate needs, to the creation of a more substantial formal enterprise providing opportunities to invest for the future.

Enterprises of this kind may include: accommodation; catering; handicraft production and retail centres; visitor centres; excursions and tours; nature, culture or rural life/village visits and experiences; and the provision of various recreation activities. This is not a definitive list. These are enterprises selling directly to tourists or tour operators. The provision of goods and services through supply chains was covered under mechanism 2 although some communities and enterprises supported though the actions identified in this section may get involved in supplying to established tourism enterprises.

Various types of enterprise model, all of which involve the poor, may be considered here. The spectrum includes:

a) Independent enterprises set up by poor individuals or families – likely to be SMEs (small or most often micro enterprises).

b) Independent enterprises as above, but linked together either geographically (e.g. in a community/ village, or on a route etc) or somehow networked.

c) Joint ventures between existing private sector enterprises and poor micro enterprises or individuals/ families.

d) Community-based enterprises which are established by communities and owned and run by them, with revenue being distributed or spent to support the community. This is sometimes referred to as CBT (community-based tourism).

e) Community-based joint venture enterprises which are joint ventures between communities and a private sector enterprises with the community having a stake and gaining benefit.

Advantages of this mechanism

- It places control in the hands of the poor.

- It helps the poor invest and develop entrepreneurship and business skills for the long term.

- It provides opportunities for future up-scaling and development.

- In some formats, revenues benefit communities more widely and can be applied to social priorities determined by them.

- It can lead to considerable transfer of skills from the established private sector to the poor.

In most developing countries, and indeed globally, many thousands of SMEs are involved in the delivery of tourism. A strategy to engage the poor in this process and to support the enterprises that result should be seen as part of the mainstream development of the sector.

Although those who establish SMEs may not be the poorest in society, the businesses they form, especially if located in poor communities, may well go on to employ very poor people and to generate revenue in those communities.

Enabling conditions

- A destination which is receiving tourist flows which can potentially grow.

- Local areas/communities with sites, heritage etc. that are potentially very attractive to tourists and also accessible.

- Community understanding about tourism and keenness to be involved in its development.

- Clear access routes to markets for new initiatives.

- Poor communities/households keen and able to acquire business skills.

- Significant support services available to assist in business planning and funding.

- Established private sector enterprises seeking genuine partnerships with poor communities for mutual benefit.

Issues and challenges

- Many basic problems face the poor in establishing and doing business.

- Tourism presents additional challenges, notably with respect to communication.

- Community expectations may be unrealistic.

- Initiatives may not be well founded and thought through.

- Leadership and distribution structures in communities may be inadequate.

- Private sector enterprises may not be seeking joint ventures.

- Agreements on joint ventures may not contain sufficient benefits and safeguards for the poor.

While successful small enterprises could deliver the greatest long term rewards, this mechanism carries some risks for the poor. There is a chance that they may put time and possibly money into activities that provide little or no return. Misguided investments could lead them into damaging debt. Sound preparation and ongoing advice and support is therefore needed.

There are a number of common, generic problems faced by the poor in setting up enterprises, which apply to tourism as well as other sectors. The main ones include: lack of capital and difficulty in obtaining credit; lack of knowledge and business skills; poor physical environment and infrastructure; and absence of insurance and other provision to cope with periods of downturn. In the field of tourism, specific challenges include poor knowledge of markets and marketing skills, language and communication issues, limited experience of handling visitors and various technical gaps and weaknesses. These challenges apply to all situations where the poor are responsible for establishing and operating the enterprise, be they individual independent businesses or community-based initiatives.

Community-based tourism (CBT) projects have been established in many destinations across all parts of the developing world. Through bringing visitors to communities, they potentially provide opportunities for significant numbers of poor people to benefit from their spending. With CBTs, the tourism activity is to some extent managed and coordinated by community institutions and there is usually a mechanism in place for at least a part of the income to be earned communally and to be used to meet specific needs identified by the community. Some CBTs have been found to have a significant economic impact, when seen within a local context, with a very high proportion of income being retained locally.[21] Social and environmental benefits can also be found, through raising awareness of the economic value of natural and cultural heritage. By providing tourists with an opportunity to see and sometimes participate in community life *in situ* they are in line with a growing market demand for authentic, meaningful experiences and interaction with local people. For these reasons, CBT has often been supported by donor agencies and NGOs promoting sustainable development. However, while some projects have been quite successful many have failed or not reached expected targets.[22]

A major problem with CBT initiatives has been difficulty in attracting visitors, owing to poor market research and not forming the offer around identified demand, poor locations that are hard to reach, lack of links to tour operators and weak marketing. Some CBT initiatives have also faced challenges of acceptance, leadership, motivation, management and equitable sharing within the community. However, with good business planning and execution, these difficulties can be avoided or addressed and the approach still has some inherent merit as outlined above.

Especially when a CBT initiative is established with the support from donor agencies or NGO's it is important to emphasize from the beginning onwards that tourism is business, and that the community should develop and run the CBT initiative as a business enterprise, making good assessments of the time and resources the community has to invest in it with the aim to achieve a positive return on investment.

In some communities the communal, CBT approach can work well, but in others it is more appropriate and successful to base development on independent SMEs, possibly working together but not sharing income. This depends partly on the traditional structure of different societies.

Box 22 Tanzania Cultural Tourism Programme[23]

This programme links together a number of communities in northern Tanzania which provide village life experiences for tourists. Services include accommodation (campsites, homestays, guesthouses), traditional food and beverages, a range of tours (e.g. village walking tours, canoeing, cycling, forest and waterfall treks), and cultural experiences (story tellers, dancing, handicraft demonstrations, preparing food). Guides come from the village and services are provided by local families, all of whom receive training.

The programme was started in 1995 by SNV and the Tanzania Tourist Board (TTB), with the latter taking over responsibility for marketing. Each community (which may include one or more villages) operates independently, but central booking is provided through the TTB information centre in Arusha. In 1996 there were 3 participating communities, rising to 17 in 2002 and 25 in 2008 with 6 in the pipeline. Visit numbers rose during this period from 600 to about 30,000 per year.

---

21   A assessment of CBT performance can be found in Spenceley, 2008b.

22   Dixey, 2005.

23   From SNV Tanzania.

The programme is delivered as a community enterprise with coordinators in each participating community. Income is received directly by individuals and households providing services but also communally through a Village Development Fee (VDF) and voluntary donations. The communal income has been used to improve local schools, health services, dispensaries, agricultural programmes and roads and provide scholarships and new tree planting schemes.

In 2007, the average number of tourists received per community was 700, delivering US$ 31,000 in total income, made up of 58% direct income to households, 11% VDF and 31% voluntary donations. In each community on average 140 people benefit from income received through providing direct services or indirect supplies, with around a further 12,000 benefitting in some way from the improvements resulting from VDF and donations. However, there are huge variations between the communities around these averages, with total income ranging from US$ 400 to US$ 270,000. Some communities are struggling to benefit from the Programme while others are doing very well. The differences relate partly to variations in quality, skill, energy, tour operator contacts and marketing and partly to location.

Challenges and lessons learned include:

- the need for continual capacity building in many functions – business management, market intelligence, IT, hospitality, food processing, languages, promotion etc.;

- strengthening the umbrella network and central marketing activity, which have been weak;

- improved, formalised legal status and access to finance;

- improved monitoring, record keeping and reporting.

A ST-EP programme running from 2008-2010 was set up to address these and other matters – using external funding to enhance and diversify the Programme, learning from the successes and failures and putting it on a sounder footing.

The basic problems of lack of capital, knowledge, technical skill, market awareness and access faced by the poor underline the advantages of engaging in joint ventures with experienced private sector operators. There are many examples of where this has worked well. A fundamental strength underpinning such arrangements is that each party provides attributes needed by the other – land, traditions, cultural and natural resources from the community; capital, business skill and market knowledge from the private enterprise.

The basis for joint ventures can vary from limited involvement of the community (perhaps just charging a rent – which comes under mechanism 5) to a revenue and profit sharing partnership and a joint business arrangement. Many tourism joint ventures have involved a whole range of benefits flowing to poor communities, from revenue or profit sharing but also from some of the other mechanisms such as direct employment of the local poor (with long term training and career development) and supply chains arrangements. In some cases, the whole enterprise is set to pass to the community after a fixed period of time. However, there are a number of issues and challenges associated with joint ventures, including ensuring that agreements truly benefit the local communities and that, within them, benefits are felt by the genuine poor.

Actions to pursue

▶ Investigate the spread of SMEs and community-based projects involving the poor

Before fixing on specific actions it is important to have a good picture of current activity. This may partly be apparent from the overall analysis of the sector in the destination, as described in section 1.4. It will be difficult to be clear about which SMEs have been established by households close to the poverty line, but some clues may be provide by knowing the communities in which they are located and the date when the enterprise started.

At the outset it is also important to be clear about the spread of public sector, NGO or donor led initiatives that are supporting sustainable development in the different communities, including those that have involved tourism and those that have not.

▶ Ensure supportive legal basis for tourism SMEs and CBT

Business related legislation and regulation should not stand in the way of SME development or setting up communal CBT structures. This also relates to issues over community rights and land tenure. This may require action to:

* Lobby for change or improvement in national legislation or its application (see section 1.1).

* Ensure sensitive and supportive local government policies and procedures.

▶ Work with stakeholders to consider and assess opportunities for new development

Opportunities for new enterprise development should be guided by the processes of product and market assessment outlined in section 1.4 and 1.5 of this manual, and the resulting strategy if one has been prepared (1.6). Further guidance is also provided in Annex 3-A. This should form the basis for:

* prioritising types of product to encourage that could be developed by SMEs or communities;

* conceiving possible new development concepts for the destination, such as themed routes, walking trails, events programmes etc., which could provide a framework for SMEs and community engagement.

Proactive interventions could start with holding discussions with stakeholders best placed to understand the needs and opportunities for development, including:

* NGOs active in the destination;

* resource ownership/management bodies such as national parks;

* private sector operators, especially incoming tour operators.

▶ Pursue and support development opportunities with individual communities

If appropriate, work could be instigated with selected individual communities.

Development work with individual communities should only be pursued if they meet certain preconditions concerning:

* awareness of the community and desire to engage in tourism;

* clear assessment of market demand, including input by tour operators, and how the market will be reached;

* inherent appeal of the location and potential visitor experience to identified markets;

* a location that is sufficiently accessible to existing and potential visitor flows;

* no threats to natural and cultural resources and social frameworks;

* high levels of safety and security for visitors.

It is important to appreciate that tourism development work with individual communities does not have to lead towards the establishment of a community-based tourism (CBT) project, with actions undertaken and income earned in common, as described earlier. While the latter is a possible option, individual households could be assisted in establishing their own enterprises and initiatives, which might be totally independent or linked with others within a broad community project.

Actions with individual communities could take a number of forms and may include some or all of the following:

- facilitated visioning, planning and project formulation exercises, as described in section 1.7 (p. 40);

- help with market and feasibility assessments of possible projects;

- coordinated work with community bodies and individual households to assist in the development and implementation of projects, possibly through a development worker under the auspices of a local NGO;

- assistance with improvement of infrastructure;

- linking in to specific technical advice and training provision (see below);

- ongoing marketing support (see below).

▶ Provide technical assistance and capacity building

There is considerable scope and need for capacity building to support poor communities and individuals seeking to establish tourism enterprises. This relates also to capacity building with existing SMEs (see section 1.7, p. 40).

Topics should be determined through local consultation but are likely to cover: general business planning and operation, marketing, communication with visitors, basic IT if appropriate, specific topics relating to hospitality, guiding etc.

Delivery may be through a combination of short training courses and ongoing access to advisory services. These could be set up either:

- on an ongoing basis or through a short term initiative; and

- for the destination as a whole or for selected areas or communities.

Trainers and advisors need to have a good understanding of the destination and of tourism. They could include:

- local NGOs or individual 'local capacity builders' who have expertise in tourism or who have established this through train-the–trainer sessions;

- private sector tourism businesses prepared to provide advice and mentoring.

Some practical pointers concerning effective training delivery were given on p. 43 and can be found in the example in box 23.

Box 23 Tourism Micro-Enterprises (METs) Project – Ecuador[24]

The objective of this project was to promote entrepreneurial development and consolidation of small and micro tourism businesses (SMEs), giving priority to those run by women and young people, through training, technical assistance and access to micro-credit. It was a ST-EP project, run jointly by UNWTO, SNV, UNDP and the Rainforest Alliance between 2006 and 2008.

To ensure tourism potential, the enterprises were selected along 8 tourist circuits, which were further identified and developed during the project. Selection involved a systematic process of following up around 150 leads, based on interviews, prior-assessment and some feasibility studies, using economic, social and environmental criteria. Eventually 87 micro-enterprises were identified, providing accommodation, food and beverage, handicrafts, guiding/transport or other services. They were in various stages of development and operation. Over half were run by women. The people involved were poor – the target was to deliver uplift in income for around 350 families.

---

24   From UNWTO ST-EP reports and project feedback.

A comprehensive programme of training and direct advice was set up for these enterprises, covering business planning and various technical subjects. It was delivered through a set of counterpart 'local economic development agencies', linked to a project coordinating committee. 25 personnel from the agencies attended a series of 'train the trainers' workshops.

Lessons learned from the process underlined the importance of the following:

- Having a number of international agencies involved, who were able to support and learn from each other.

- Selecting the right local counterpart agencies, who played a critical role. They should show at the outset: good initial knowledge of the subject (subsequently complemented by 'train the trainers'); full commitment of time by the designated personnel; good knowledge of the local area and key players there; experience of training adults.

- Having standard agreed criteria for the selection of microenterprises, partly to orientate the local agencies in this process and ensure transparency. The enterprises selected should ideally be all at a similar level and face similar challenges.

- Making sure all enterprises have accurate understanding and expectations about the programme and what they will get out of it.

- Paying attention to logistical details concerning workshops etc. – location, timing, access, venue, facilities.

- Tailoring training to local needs – devoting most time to the important subjects; not relying on IT if the enterprises have no computer access; providing personal supervision in the preparation of business plans by each enterprise.

▶ Promote and facilitate the establishment of joint ventures

The considerable benefits that poor communities can gain from joint ventures/ partnerships with established private sector businesses suggests that in general these should be actively encouraged. While this is primarily up to the parties concerned, action can be taken to help to make links and facilitate agreements, in order to ensure that the poor gain full advantage of their position. Public bodies and especially NGOs at the destination level may be well placed to provide objective support, respected by both sides.

This could include:

- encouraging existing tourism enterprises to consider partnership arrangements;

- empowering communities – ensuring that they are fully aware of their rights;

- helping private sector enterprises who wish to develop in the destination find sites and reach beneficial agreements with local communities;

- assisting local communities find and select private sector partners to work with them on tourism development and marketing (see box 24);

- providing guidelines on the contents of agreements;

- providing legal support and representation for local communities in negotiating agreements;

- overseeing and monitoring agreements and ensuring that they are complied with;

- minimising bureaucracy and delays in official procedures.

Agreements between the parties should be clear and unambiguous. They should include obligations on the private operator to take specified actions which benefit the poor and allow access to land and other resources in ways that do not threaten local livelihoods.

Box 24 Examples of joint venture arrangements

Community-based ecotourism in Anjozorobe-Angave Protected Area, Madagascar[25]

This ST-EP supported project has both environmental and poverty-alleviation objectives. A local NGO, Fanamby, has been working with the local community on the development of a range of tourism offers, centred on the establishment of an ecolodge at the entrance to the reserve consisting of 10 bungalows. An innovative management scheme has been introduced in order on the one hand to ensure quality services and on the other to enable the community to profit economically.

A sustainable tourism code was drawn up with the community, concerning the impacts of tourism and the benefits sought. This has formed the basis for selection of a professional private sector management company to run the lodge, which remains in the ownership of the community. Three companies submitted tenders, which were evaluated by a committee of the local community, with the assistance of Fanamby. The winning company demonstrated the best professional experience, market contacts, local knowledge and understanding of the community's objectives. The contract agreement clearly sets out the obligations of the management company and the owner (the community) and includes specifications concerning financial returns to the community, the employment of local people and local sourcing of supplies. The company has also been involved with a local training programme in the community.

Pafuri camp, South Africa[26]

This high quality ecotourism facility is an outcome of a three way partnership between the Makuleke community, Kruger National Park (South Africa National Parks), and an experienced private operator Wilderness Safaris. The community owns the land and provides the majority of staffing, SANParks provides infrastructure, public sector endorsement and conservation expertise, and Wilderness Safaris provides finance and experience of tourism and marketing. In the first years following opening the community earned around US$ 130,000 from revenue share and US$ 400,000 from salaries for the 54 local people employed. The partnership works around a set of very carefully drafted agreements, with collective decisions being taken by a Joint Management Board.

▶ Promote and facilitate the availability of funding

The significant problem of lack of capital for investment by SME developers can be addressed through various options for the provision of financial assistance, including subsidies and facilitating the chances of good schemes obtaining credit.

It has been found that often the problem, especially in the area of loan finance, is not so much the existence of accessible funding but the quality of schemes put forward.[27] A fundamental issue is the economic sustainability of projects seeking finance, with a concern for social and environmental sustainability also being increasingly shown by financing bodies. Assistance at destination level is relevant here as projects are more likely to be considered favourably for funding if:

- they are seen to be in line with a realistic destination strategy;

- they are well formulated – possibly as the result of input of technical assistance to help with business planning and market assessment.

---

25   From UNWTO ST-EP reports and project feedback.
26   From World Tourism Organization, 2009.
27   World Tourism Organization, 2005b.

An approach. frequently adopted by SNV, is to provide technical assistance to enterprises through training sessions and workshops, and then to help link these enterprises with sources of finance.

As well as influencing the quality of applications, action can also be taken in the destination on improving the availability of finance. Alternative approaches could include:

- Working with microfinance institutions (MFIs) that have a presence in the destination. Selected MFIs could be encouraged to take a specialist interest in tourism projects and build up a good understanding of their needs, as a lack of knowledge of the sector is often a problem with MFIs. These MFIs could also engage in delivering technical assistance to client enterprises to underpin their loans and gain leverage from them. Box 25 provides an individual example of this. The METs programme (box 23) also undertook a detailed study of local MFIs and provided guidance materials for stakeholders on access to microfinance for tourism.

- Parcelling up external funding, e.g. from international donors, and making it available in small amounts to applicants in the destination, linked to specific criteria, and administered through a local NGO or dedicated body. This could be continued over time as a revolving fund. Another form of intervention is for third party organizations to guarantee loans on behalf of the poor.

Box 25 Zakoura Foundation for Microcredit, Morocco[28]

This MFI has become a specialist in tourism micro-enterprises through its Rural Tourism Programme, which gives loan of between US$ 500 and 5,000, and has supported over 1,000 projects in five years since its inception in 2003. It is delivered by 8 loan officers working across five rural areas. Tourism was chosen as a relatively low risk opportunity for taking microcredit into rural areas. To support this, the Foundation has developed particular expertise in the subject which has enabled it to focus on what is realistic in the marketplace. Zakoura has created its own capacity building activity and the loan officers have played a very important role in advising clients. It has also established its own certification programme, covering quality but also sustainability including various requirements relating to the local community and economy.

▶ Encourage and support networking between enterprises

The formation of associations or loose networks between SMEs of the same type and between CBTs can help to overcome problems related to their small size and fragmentation. Networks, which could be formed within destinations or nationally, can help to:

- raise their profile generally and in the market place;

- encourage mutual learning and sharing of experiences;

- provide a basis for ongoing capacity building and assistance;

- plan joint marketing activities and operate a joint booking centre;

- facilitate links with similar enterprises in other destinations and countries.

A number of countries have seen the establishment of associations supporting SMEs and CBTs, but with mixed success. Problems with the economic sustainability of such associations point to the need for them to:

- clearly demonstrate economic value from market-facing activity; and

- be based on sound business models, with committed support and funding from members and from public sector bodies.

---

28   From World Tourism Organization, 2005b plus updated information.

▶ Ensure and actively deliver effective marketing

This is fundamental to the success of SMEs and CBTs and a reason for many failures. Much can be done at a destination level, including:

- Forging links to tour operators. In-country handling agents and international tour operators (both of whom influence itinerary planning) should be encouraged to visit and use SMEs and CBTs, including providing them with information and organising familiarisation trips. Ideally, links with tour operators should already be established during the initial stages of developing SMEs and CBTs, to ask for feedback on the proposed products and ensure the SMEs and CBTs meet the needs of the tour operators. This can also motivate the tour operators to cooperate with the SMEs and CBTs, as they have been engaged with the SMEs and CBTs from the early stages of developing their products.

- Incorporating in destination marketing. Destination (and where appropriate, national) websites and print should give strong exposure to:

  - themes, types of tourism and locations which are most likely to involve SMEs and CBTs;

  - specific CBT and SME products.

- Helping individual products with internet exposure. Some products could be directly exposed to markets through the creation of simple dedicated websites or through securing presence on selected third party sites promoting relevant products and with appropriate booking procedures.

- Generating media coverage. Press releases and media liaison should put over messages and stories related to these themes and products, to both international and domestic media. A particular effort should be made to ensure that relevant information is supplied to guidebook writers so they can make use of this when updating their pages on the destination.

- Assisting with promotional initiatives. Simple information may not be enough to draw attention to relevant themes, locations and products. Assistance could be given for the mounting of special events and pursuing other innovative ideas.

- Improving local information and signposting. Every effort should be made to ensure that tourists in the area know what it is available to them. Relevant action includes: providing information through hotels, guides etc.; establishing tourist information centres; and providing and maintaining effective signposting.

▶ Promote the equitable sharing of benefits within communities

Many CBTs and joint ventures, and some kinds of SMEs, will generate income not only for the enterprises themselves but also communal income for use within communities. Actions to promote the equitable sharing of such income and deliver benefits to people most in need are relevant here but covered in detail under mechanism 5.

2.4 Considering the enterprise development mechanism

1   Based on your analysis of tourism in the destination, think about what you know about tourism related SMEs or CBTs.

  - How prevalent are SMEs of CBTs in your destination?

  - Are you aware of attempts by poor communities or individual households to establish tourism enterprises and the barriers and problems that they face?

  - Are there any barriers provided by legislation, local bureaucracy etc.?

2 Consider the assessment of product and market opportunities in the destination and your tourism strategy. What kinds of themes and products have you identified and prioritised? What opportunities do you think these present for local communities and SMEs? Should you talk further to NGOs, tour operators and other stakeholders?

3 Are there particular communities which could benefit from an integrated approach to tourism development? How can this be instigated and supported?

4 Who is best placed to deliver training and advice for tourism SME development in the destination? Is it necessary to 'train the trainers'?

5 Are you aware of private sector operators/developers looking to establish themselves or expand in the destination, who could form joint ventures with poor communities? Are there communities looking for joint venture partners? Who could best help in securing effective agreements?

6 Are there Microfinance Institutions supporting SME development in the destination – could they do more to support tourism? Could a dedicated fund be set up to support tourism SMEs or CBTs?

7 Does the destination have a website and promotional print? If so, are relevant themes and products covered in this? Could you do more to promote these to tour operators, the media, guidebook publishers etc? Is there adequate local visitor information and signposting for tourists in the area?

2.5 Tax or Charge on Tourists or Enterprises

This is about using for poverty alleviation the money raised from tourism through general taxation or a more specific charge. It covers compulsory charges – voluntary donation is covered under Mechanism 6. There are various different manifestations of this mechanism, as described below.

- **Overall business taxation in the tourism sector.** One of the most significant ways in which tourism can assist poverty alleviation is through the wealth it generates for the national exchequer through the general taxation of tourism businesses and the subsequent use of this wealth on social and poverty alleviation programmes.

- **More specific taxes or charges collected generally from tourists or tourism enterprises.** Some specific taxes or charges may be levied by government on activities that relate particularly to tourism. These include, for example, visa fees and airport charges. They also include bed taxes, collected per person per night, which are raised nationally or locally in some countries. Again, revenue from these charges may be used for poverty alleviation.

- **Charges made on tourists for a particular activity.** These are site or area specific charges, and include, for example, admission fees to national parks or other public or community amenities. Revenue raised could be used to benefit the welfare of communities in the area.

- **Charges made on tourism enterprises or developers for a particular resource or benefit.** These include licence fees, concession charges or rental payments to develop or operate in an area or on a particular site. They may be paid to public sector bodies, with the revenue possibly used for social purposes, or paid to communities.

The above approaches are not mutually exclusive and all of them could be found in a destination.

There is a relationship between the last two types of charge and topics covered in the last section under mechanism 4 – enterprise development. Where a charge is made to tourists for a visitor experience actively provided by a community, such as a village visit, this might be seen more accurately as the development of an enterprise that charges a price to visitors for the service offered. Where a community receives a rental payment from a private developer and is in any way involved with the resulting tourism operation, this could be seen more positively as a joint tourism venture.

Advantages of this mechanism

- Because the incidence of taxation and compulsory charging can fall on large numbers of people, quite significant resources can be raised in this way.

- The mechanism can theoretically enable all poor people to benefit from tourism, without having to be involved in any way in the tourism sector.

- Revenue raised can be directed at the poorest in society and at key social need such as health care.

- It can involve quite simple mechanisms of collection.

Enabling conditions

- Sufficient tourism activity in the county and/or destination to generate a tax base.

- Sound governance with fair and efficient handling of fiscal processes.

- High priority given to poverty alleviation in public spending.

- Poor communities who can benefit from revenue raised from tourism taxes.

- The existence of some sites, such as national parks, at which a charge can be made in return for access or other tourist experiences.

- Effective and transparent mechanisms for raising charges and disbursing revenues.

- Enterprises and tourists prepared to comply with taxes and charges.

Issues and challenges

- Tourists and tourism enterprises may be put off from coming or spending if taxes are too high.

- In some countries poor governance, corruption, inefficiency and lack of transparency can be major problems.

- Tourists and enterprises may not fully understand the reason for taxes and charges.

- It may be difficult to ensure that money raised actually reaches poor communities rather than being spent in other ways.

- Payments made to communities may not be equitably shared within them and benefit the most needy.

This mechanism can be quite controversial and raises some rather fundamental questions concerning the relationship between achieving social objectives and maintaining the competitiveness of the tourism sector. It is very important that any taxes and charges on tourists do not prevent them from coming and spending money in the destination, nor must they threaten the viability of tourism enterprises. Striking the right balance is important.

It can be a challenge to persuade governments to earmark the revenues from particular national taxes for uses on specific purposes. Once revenue is received by the Exchequer it is normally beyond reach of further influence and is put towards priority spending programmes. However, in most developing countries these are most likely to include overall poverty alleviation, not least because of the need to comply with global commitments.

The efficient and equitably raising and spending of tax revenues depends on good and fair governance. This is a problem at a national and local level in some countries meaning that monies raised do not reach the intended beneficiaries.

It can be easier to link taxes and charges raised locally to specific local causes. This provides opportunities to communicate and demonstrate these causes directly to visiting tourists and to involve communities in decisions on the use of funds raised.

A number of studies have demonstrated that often tourists are quite willing to pay compulsory charges or levies if there is a good reason to do so. This willingness appears to be strongest when:

- careful explanations are given as to why charges are being made and about the beneficial causes to which they will be put; and

- it is clearly necessary to make a payment, which could be quite a large sum, in order to visit a place or undertake an activity that is high on the tourist's list of priorities.

The example from Tanzania, illustrated in box 5 on p. 22 showed the very considerable National Park entrance fees for the Kilimanjaro trek, accounting for 47% of the cost per visitor, which people appear to be prepared to pay in order to have this special experience. However, it was impossible to determine exactly what this was used for and how much benefitted the poor.

Lack of transparency about the use of taxes and charges is a challenge found in many places. It is important to address this as tourists and tourism enterprises do need to know how their contributions are being spent.

Where revenues from taxes and charges are failing to reach the poor, it should not be assumed that this can be easily adjusted. Often, such revenues are highly important as income sources for other activities – for example in providing essential core funding for a national park service and its conservation work.

A different sort of challenge concerns circumstances where a charge should be levied but this is not happening. Sometimes tour operators and tourists are, knowingly or unknowingly, exploiting local communities. A common example is where tourists are taken to poor villages or to traditional cultural sites but the community is not benefiting from this at all. More broadly, there may be a need to review the level of rental or other compensation paid by tourism enterprise for the use of community land and resources.

Finally there may be issues with the process of agreeing on and reaching beneficiaries of revenues actually within poor communities. Equity and transparency can be lacking at this level. Sometimes, traditional practices and hierarchical structures can mean that resources do not reach or benefit those that need them most.

These issues can be quite hard to address at a destination level, but a number of relevant actions are outlined below.

Actions to pursue

▶ **Clarify the amount and use of tourism-related tax revenues collected and lobby for their use on local poverty alleviation**

Having an understanding of the amount of money contributed by the tourism sector in the destination to both national and local taxation is helpful politically in adding weight to arguments about the importance of tourism. This information could be used to seek to influence national and local government activities in the destination.

Relevant actions include:

* Working out approximately the contribution to national and local tax revenues from tourism businesses and visitor spending in the destination.

* Clarifying the use of any revenues from tourism related charges such as visa fees and lobbying for transparency over this, including possible use of funds for poverty alleviation and pro-poor tourism support in local areas.

* Lobbying local government on the use of local taxation revenue (including any specific levies such as bed taxes) to support local pro-poor tourism and poverty alleviation schemes.

Box 26 Bhutan tourism charging[29]

The Royal Government of Bhutan operates an unusual system of centralised charging for all international tourists: a minimum tourist tariff of US$ 200 per person per day (with seasonal discounts and variations) is set by the government for an all-inclusive package. Following the subtraction of any offshore agent's commission (typically 10%) the remainder of the tariff is paid into a bank account managed by the Tourism Council of Bhutan. Tour operators are then paid from this account after several additional deductions have been made.

These deductions comprise a US$ 65 government royalty and a 2% tax on the remaining balance. The royalty provides an important source of income for health, education and other local development programmes. For example, it is estimated that the royalty and other taxes paid by the tourism industry represented 4% of the country's revenue in 2004. The national revenue of US$ 115 million in 2004 was spent on free health and education programmes for Bhutan's citizens (17%), nature conservation (11%) and other local development programmes (30%).[30]

In addition, a further US$ 10 from every tourist visiting the country (more for tourists in groups of two or less) is allocated to a 'Tourism Development Fund' (TDF). The fund was established in 2000 as a way to help facilitate the sustainable development of the tourism industry and to promote participation by all stakeholders. In general, the fund is seen as a useful mechanism for allocating budget for sustainable tourism development activities where government budget and private sector investment are not sufficient.

A change in the way the TDF is managed is under consideration to identify opportunities to better ensure the equitable distribution of the fund among tourism stakeholders, and to further clarify issues relating to the ownership and transparency of the fund. Further reform – which has been proposed in the past - could help to improve the effectiveness of the fund even more.

While the government is determined to maintain the tourism royalty, it does recognise that a minimum daily tariff may not necessarily be the most sustainable solution for tourism development in the long run. An increase in the royalty, while doing away with the daily tariff to allow the private sector to improve its performance, would be a possible option to address certain sustainability issues (including a number of tour operators which currently undercut the daily tariff).

▶ Improve transparency and use of current compulsory charging at sites and locations in the destination

Consideration should be given to all locations and situations where tourists are currently being asked to pay a charge – this may include, for example: admissions to national parks or historic sites, charges of use of infrastructure, such as road tolls, and visits to villages.

In each case, action should be taken to:

* identify the extent to which revenue from the charge is being retained in the local destination and being used to benefit the poor;

---

29   From SNV Bhutan.

30   Rinzin et al., 2007.

- encourage engagement with local communities over the use of revenues;

- increase the proportion of revenues that is used channelled to poor communities and used on poverty alleviation;

- strengthen monitoring and reporting on this;

- review and improve information provided to tourists and tour operators on the use of the charge.

Some further points about beneficiary projects and how to communicate with tourists are provided in section 2.6.

▶ Consider additional charging possibilities and pursue if appropriate

Various options for consideration and investigation include:

- increasing the levels of charge at sites/locations where this is already happening;

- introducing charges for some additional locations and activities. In particular, any situations where visits are being made by tourists but the local community is not benefiting should be identified;

- introducing a standard charge on tourists. An example is a local bed tax, charged per person per night on occupied hotels rooms or other accommodation, which may be paid by the establishment or passed on to tourists. This is quite common in some countries but is often disliked by businesses as they see it as a threat to their competitiveness.

In each case, beneficiary communities and causes, together with structures and processes for delivering funds to them, should be clear before proceeding. Transparency and good communication should be a natural feature of any new schemes.

A critical next step is to consult fully with local stakeholders before any changes are made. This should include local tourism enterprises, tour operators, affected public bodies and local communities.

If possible research should be undertaken amongst visitors about willingness to pay. Previous experience suggests that they may be more positive about this than tourism enterprises. Variation in response between different types of visitor should be probed. An example of a simple research exercise is given in box 27.

Box 27 Willingness to Pay study, Sa Pa District, Viet Nam[31]

Sa Pa is a district of great beauty but also poverty in north west Viet Nam. The ethnic minority communities and their cultural sites are a primary attraction for tourists. Previously a haphazard system was in place for tourists to make very small payments at a number of collection points in the area. However, stakeholders concerned with poverty alleviation decided that there was an opportunity to increase the revenue raised to benefit the communities by increasing increase the charge and asking for a single payment from all visitors. Before making any changes it was decided that this must be researched.

In 2001 a small survey was undertaken over four days interviewing visitors in Sa Pa using questionnaires. A 'contingent valuation' method was adopted to test willingness to pay, using bidding-style questions – essentially probing how high they would be prepared to go. Considerable differences were found in the levels indicated by international visitors (US$ 4) and Vietnamese (US$ 1.5 to US$ 2). All visitors stressed that they would need to be told where the money was going if they were to be happy about making these payments. Options for the use of funds were tested – the one most favoured was "support for general ethnic minority projects, including schools and healthcare". The study recommended fixing the charge at US$ 2 – at the top end of the domestic visitor range.

---

31 Deen, 2001.

> Local tourism enterprises were also interviewed. This revealed a stark contrast with the positive attitude shown by tourists. The operators were almost all very opposed to the payments and felt they should be scrapped rather than raised. They clearly had very little knowledge of the current system and saw all payments as a penalty rather than a way of delivering benefit. This underlined the need for transparency and awareness raising.

▶ **Ensure maximum pro-poor benefit is obtained from granting of licences, leases and concessions to tourism enterprises**

Governments can raise revenue from tourism enterprises, or from developers, through annual fees in return for the granting of licenses, leases or concessions to develop or operate on government owned land. This income can, in turn, be used to benefit poor communities, either in the locations in question or more generally. This very much depends on how the national or local government agencies concerned chose to use the money. Similarly, communities with rights of ownership can gain income directly through this process.

Simply raising revenue in this way can provide a valuable mechanism for benefiting the poor. However, it is important to see this alongside the wider benefits that can be leveraged from concession agreements, through requiring the formation of joint ventures, provision of local employment etc. as discussed in the section 2.4.

In South Africa, South Africa National Parks received US$ 15 million in 2007 from concessions, rentals etc. in its parks. However, it sees the main beneficial result from its commercialisation strategy as being the "ability to reduce poverty in remote areas through the creation of sustainable employment" , which is a result of the leverage requirements it places on concessions. See box 9, p. 42.

▶ **Establish objective and transparent structures for receipt and equitable deployment of revenues, generally and within communities**

In order to achieve effective, targeted poverty alleviation in the destination, there is a need to ensure that revenues generated from taxes and charges find their way to the poor. This applies also to revenues obtained through community enterprises (mechanism 4) and voluntary giving (Mechanism 6). Income from these mechanisms should be targeted at those at most in need, directly or through the provision of services that can most benefit them (such as water schemes, health care etc.) given that they enable such flexibility compared with those mechanisms that require active participation by the poor in tourism.

Action could be taken at two levels.

- **In the destination as a whole.** It may be appropriate to work through the local authority(ies) or one or more NGOs. Alternatively, a dedicated **foundation or trust** could be established, specifically for the receipt and dispersal of resources raised through tourism (from tourists, tourism enterprises, related charges etc.). This could be facilitated through participating NGOs, who would play an essential role in identifying beneficiary causes. It should be steered by a committee which includes representation from the tourism industry (tour operators and service enterprises) to help in securing goodwill from the sector. This body should be responsible for effective reporting and communication to ensure transparency.

- **In individual communities.** A significant part of the revenues may be raised within or specifically targeted at individual communities. It will be necessary to ensure that transparent structures are in place at this level, which respect traditional community structures but are not dictated by them. Links with a destination level foundation could be established.

Box 28 Transparent arrangements in Luang Namtha, Lao PDR[32]

In northern Laos the Nam Ha Ecotourism Project worked with a variety of local stakeholders to establish a tourism product involving trekking, village visits and other experiences. Great care was taken to set up and implement an agreed system for distributing economic benefits equitably within the communities.

Figures from the Nam Ha Ecoguide Service, a community based tour operator, illustrate the process. Looking at the gross revenue from tours, 72% was paid directly to local people providing services (accommodation, food, guiding and handicrafts) based on agreed, standardised and fare rates. The remainder was dispersed through a series of taxes and charges, which both support the tourism operation and benefit the community. These included:

- Tourism Promotion Fund. A 5% levy applied to all tours and used for marketing the destination.

- Village Development Fund. An 8% premium on the price of each tour, managed by the Provincial Tourism Department and used to assist projects proposed by the villages including clean water, basic infrastructure, environmental programmes etc. Use must be approved by the governor.

- Trekking permit. A US$ 1 flat charge per person per day used to fund conservation.

- Provincial tax (on business). Normally 10% on value added, but this can be significantly reduced if the business pledges to support the Village Development Fund.

2.5 Considering the tax or charge mechanism

1 Consider the process of taxation on tourism enterprises nationally and locally, including any specific charges and fees levied on tourism. Do you think this is contributing to poverty alleviation? Do you see possibilities to lobby for allocating a larger percentage of these charge for poverty alleviation?

2 In your destination, are there locations where tourists pay an admission or equivalent charge to visit a park, heritage site etc.? Do you know what happens to this money and whether it helps neighbouring poor communities? Are tourists made aware of this?

3 Think whether more charges could or should be made in your destination.

   – Are there situations where tourists or tour operators are visiting locations where the local community is not benefitting?

   – Do you know what tour operators and tourists feel about paying charges?

4 Could more benefit be obtained through granting concessions, leases etc. – Where and by whom?

5 How can you ensure that revenues raised in this way reach the genuine poor? Are local community structures equitable and transparent? Would a new dedicated foundation or trust at a destination level be helpful?

---

32 Schipani, 2008.

2.6 Voluntary Giving by Tourists or Tourism Enterprises

This is about the voluntary giving of money or other forms of assistance to poor individuals or communities by tourists or tourism enterprises. This may be used to:

- support directly a wide range of beneficiary causes, such as health care, clinics, water supplies, infrastructure, schools, scholarships and bursaries, etc.;

- assist in the development of enterprise and activities, which may include tourism as one of the possible sectors.

Giving by tourists may involve:

- Financial donations, made before, during or after the visit. They could be made in a variety of ways, such as:

  - A small donation made by a tourist when visiting a site or community.

  - A small voluntary supplement that may be added to a payment, for example at the request of a tour operator when booking a tour.

  - A sizeable financial contribution or personal sponsorship, which may be made once or be continued over many years after the visit.

- Provision of non-financial gifts, skill, labour, information and cultural exchange. This may occur:

  - On an ad hoc basis during a trip.

  - Through participating in an organised working holiday or visit. 'Volunteer tourism[33]' is a sizeable and growing market sector.

Giving by tourism enterprises may involve:

- Provision of money in the form of corporate donations or sponsorships. This may entail a one-off payment or a long term commitment.

- A direct and deep involvement with one or more communities, which may be local to the enterprise in question (if a service provider such as a lodge or hotel) or regularly visited by them (if a tour operator). Giving may support a wide range of activity affecting all aspects of community wellbeing.

The latter form of voluntary giving by a tourism enterprise is often intertwined with joint venture enterprise development (mechanism 4) and the provision of employment (Mechanism 1) and may involve collateral benefits to communities (mechanism 7). The enterprise's motives and actions may be an indivisible mixture of:

- commercial – seeing community giving as underpinning its long term business position and enhancing its market profile; and

- philanthropic – giving for strongly felt altruistic reasons, and also providing employment and skills etc., partly for these reasons as well.

Giving by tourists and by tourism enterprises is sometimes linked, with one stimulating the other. An enterprise may pledge to match its clients' contributions, for example.

Giving may be directed quite generally, to schemes or NGOs with widespread initiatives and clients, or focused on individual communities or very specific projects.

---

33   Volunteer tourists have been defined as those who 'volunteer in an organised way to undertake holidays that may involve alleviating the material poverty of some groups in society, the restoration of certain environments, or research into aspects of society or environment' (Lyons and Wearing, 2008).

Advantages of this mechanism

- It enables money and other benefits to be targeted at very specific causes, which may benefit the poorest and most needy.

- Substantial sums of money can be raised in this way, often with few delays and barriers.

- It raises awareness of poverty issues amongst tourists, enterprises and more widely.

- It can help to foster positive relations between visitors, tourism and local communities.

- It can supplement income earned from commercial tourism activity, often at the same time.

The experience of the Tanzania Cultural Tourism Programme (box 22, p. 73) which found 31% of total income coming from donations, illustrates the relative importance of the mechanism in providing supplementary benefit.

Enabling conditions

- The presence of tourists who are willing to support local causes.

- Tourism enterprises (tour operators and service providers) who are keen to facilitate and encourage voluntary giving.

- Clearly identifiable, interesting beneficiary projects and causes which can be well described capture tourists' imagination.

- Effective and transparent mechanisms for collecting and disbursing donations.

Issues and challenges

- Some may see this process as static and patronising, creating dependency rather and assisting self-help.

- Communities may not feel fully involved with it.

- The projects supported may be superficial and not sustainable.

- Monies raised my not reach the intended beneficiaries.

- Collection and dispersal mechanism may be costly and absorb too much of the money raised.

Tourism is a unique activity in the special awareness and interaction it creates between people with money and many material resources and those with few. There are opportunities to gain further benefit from voluntary giving, but this needs to be tackled sensitively.

The mechanism is open to criticism as a form of static charity, creating dependency rather than delivering sustainable benefit. However, this depends on how the money and other support are used. Voluntary giving can be used to strengthen the capacity of the poor, through supporting education and the transfer of skills, as well as addressing immediate social needs.

The selection of beneficiary projects, how the money is handled, and how the whole process is communicated both to the givers and the receivers, is very important.

This should be genuine and transparent on both sides.

Trust and commitment are required to underpin this mechanism. Money must reach the intended beneficiaries and be seen to do so. Communities should feel involved in the process. Likewise, it is important to avoid token gestures, which may be no more than conscience-salving by tourists and the industry.

It is important to selecting beneficiary causes that are genuine priorities in terms of poverty alleviation. This may not always coincide with those that would naturally be selected by tourism enterprises and tourists. Some objective involvement by NGOs may be helpful for this reason amongst others.

The merits of volunteer tourism have been the subject of recent debate. Critics suggest the volunteers may obtain a rewarding and enjoyable experience while poor communities see little lasting benefit. However, this does not have to be the case and there are examples of significant impact being achieved. Much depends on the programme, the preparation and attention to detail.

Actions to pursue

▶ **Encourage tourism enterprises to support neighbouring local communities**

Actions taken by individual tourism enterprises to build a strong, supportive relationship with their neighbouring local communities is one of the most effective and sustainable ways of reaching the poor through tourism. Voluntary giving should be a part of this alongside the various other mechanisms described in this manual.

Examples of some of the philanthropic activity of individual enterprises are provided in box 29.

There are many examples where private sector tourism enterprises have established their own foundations involving local communities. This foundation then oversees the receiving and use of donations (corporate and from guests) and external grants as well as joint venture projects.

These actions are really in the hands of the enterprises themselves, but the process can be encouraged at a destination level through:

- encouraging enterprise to report on their activities, share experiences and spur each other on;

- awarding and publicising good practice;

- removing bureaucratic barriers and securing linkages to related schemes supported by the public sector or NGOs (e.g. in health, education etc.).

Box 29 Examples of projects supported by tourism enterprises and tourists

Jungle Bay Resort and Spa, Dominica, West Indies[34] created the Jungle Bay Community Fund. This has provided micro loans, scholarships to students, conservation education, support for local health centres and a water system for the neighbouring village. In 2007 the owners, staff and guests raised US$ 20,000 as a seed grant for the development of The House of Hope, a community operated facility for indigenous children with severe disabilities. This stimulated the government of Dominica to donated land for the project and significant contributions from several other entities in the local area, bringing the total to US$ 50,000 from Jungle Bay affiliated sources. Lessons learned included the need for a bottom-up approach which is community and staff driven, and the need to appreciate that programmes take time and patience.

Turtle Island, Fiji[35] an up-market resort, created the Yasawas Community Foundation as a mechanism for generating guest donations and ensuring that they are applied to projects which provide real solutions to real problems facing local residents. Projects have included an innovative approach to healthcare, including establishing a local eye clinic which has tackled a traditional problem of cataracts leading to blindness in the community. Turtle Island has also fostered and mentored the local community in the development of community-run backpacker accommodation on the islands.

---

34   From presentation at Travelers' Philanthropy Conference, Arusha, Tanzania 2008.
35   Fact Sheet from The Conference Board, New York, 2002.

Phinda Private Game Reserve, South Africa[36] gives high priority to social impact and poverty alleviation. They couple strategic philanthropy with other ways of working with poor communities, including employment provision and local procurement. The parent company CCAfrica set up a special NGO, Africa Foundation, to undertake work for the communities. This is supported by a wide variety of individual and institutional donors. The projects they have supported include extensive provision for:

- schools – e.g. 90 classrooms built, 150,000 books supplied and numerous other initiatives;

- health care – e.g. 2 clinics created, HIV training workshops, boreholes, water rollers;

- skills and training – e.g. built a market and trained the committee, trained 35 artisans, 86 bursaries provided.

▶ Establish a framework for coordinating voluntary giving in the destination

Voluntary giving, by tourists and enterprises, could be more effective if it was better coordinated at a destination level. The idea of establishing a system using selected existing NGOs and/or establishing a dedicated foundation or trust was suggested in section 2.5 (p. 81). A structure of this kind could be used to promote voluntary giving by:

- building up a portfolio of high priority projects in need of support, both destination-wide and in local communities;

- identifying tourism enterprises that may be interested in extending their philanthropic activity, including those who may not have formed a relationship with a specific local community – e.g. tour operators bring tourists into the area;

- matchmaking beneficiary projects with potential supporters;

- developing specific schemes to enable and encourage individual tourists to support these causes;

- facilitating transparent distribution of donations received.

In several countries, hotels have started collaborating with NGOs or the Government to set up schemes to encourage their guests to make a contribution to a poverty reduction or biodiversity conservation project. For example, a leaflet or information note is left in each hotel room, inviting the guests to make a US$ 1.00 donation a night to the project. The leaflet can mention that this donation will be charged to the final guest's account, and indicate that in case the guest does not want to participate, he can advise the cashier at the moment of settling the account. It is likely that in this way a far higher amount can be collected, then when guests would be asked to leave a voluntary contribution in a donation box at the reception. For the hotel, it is more interesting to establish such a donation scheme than to add a US$ 1.00 charge (development fee) to the room night, as the donation does not increase the actual room rate.

▶ Strengthen communication with tourists about voluntary giving

The amount of money that can be raised through voluntary giving is very sensitive to the communication process adopted. The psychology of giving has been studied and practical guidance extracted from this.[37] A strategy for improved communication on this subject in the destination should include:

- providing tourists with helpful guidance on how to handle being approached for money and gifts (such as on-street begging) as well as ways of giving money;

- encouraging tour operators and guides to talk to their groups about giving. Gentle personal influence backed by information and answering questions can be by far the most effective approach;

---

36   Presentation by The African Safari Lodge Foundation, 2008.
37   Work in the field of tourism includes Ham, 2009.

- facilitating visits to beneficiary projects, such as schools, as part of visitor programmes;

- including information about giving in tourist information material;

- encouraging ongoing links and communication between the projects and the tourist who has given support, reporting back on how this has been used.

A key to success is selecting the right projects and putting over the right messages about them. This should include:

- giving assurance that all the money will be used directly on the project and not be subject to large overhead payments;

- focussing the giving and the messages on specific, practical, understandable outcomes – describing clearly how the money will be used and how past donations have already been used;

- making it easy and practical for visitors to donate – they are much more likely to do so if they know exactly what to do;

- possibly giving some guidance about the range of donations that might be appropriate – for example indicating what can be achieved by a donation of a certain amount.

▶ Improve communities' awareness and understanding of voluntary giving

Communities seeking to benefit from visitors should be helped in the effective use of voluntary giving. This should include provision of training and advice in the community covering:

- whether or not this is an appropriate mechanism for the community, including whether to set something up locally or to rely on wider destination level mechanisms;

- the selection of projects and communication approaches to adopt, reflecting the points made above;

- awareness raising generally in the community about the giving process, including work with adults and children to address issues of begging and hassling of visitors – linking this to the alternative approaches that may have been put in place, such as a village charge (Mechanism 5) or organised giving scheme.

▶ Encourage the development of 'volunteer tourism' schemes that are truly beneficial

This specific form of tourism programme can be helpful if handled well.[38] Opportunities may exist for developing volunteer tourism in the destination or strengthening it if it is already happening. It is important to work with agencies who are experienced and able to handle this professionally. Requirements include:

- having organisers in the destination who build a very strong relationship with the host community – ensuring that the tasks are genuinely valuable to them and really well set up;

- ensuring excellent links between the international operators who recruit volunteers and the local organisers;

- detailed briefing of volunteers before departure, effective orientation on arrival and debriefing afterwards so that the process can be continually strengthened from experience;

- agreeing written memorandums of understanding between recipient communities and operators so everyone knows their responsibilities.

---

38   Findings from research specifically on this subject are contained in Lyons and Wearing, 2008.

Box 30 Niall Mellon Township Trust [39]

This trust was established in Ireland and South Africa in 2002. It is now the largest charity provider of homes in South African townships. Poverty in the county is exacerbated by poor housing – 4.3 million (11% of the population) live in informal shacks. The Trust has 80 full time and many hundreds of sub-contracted local staff, but a large amount of input comes from thousands of volunteers who travel as tourists to South Africa to build the homes. Each volunteer has to raise over US$ 6,000 to participate, half of which covers their flights and living expenses on site but the other half is used on materials for the house building. Just over 2,000 volunteers can build 250 homes, providing housing for 1,500 people after one week. The Trust is also involved in community development work and social programmes.

 **2.6 Considering the voluntary giving mechanism**

1 Are you aware of tourism enterprises which are engaged in voluntary projects with their local communities? Are others in the industry aware of what some of their peers are doing? Is this publicised enough?

2 Is there a need for more coordination of voluntary giving in the destination? What do local NGOs think about this?

3 Could opportunities for giving be better communicated to visitors? Is this covered in visitor information?

4 Is there much begging and hassling of visitors in the destination? Could more be done to help local communities and visitors handle this better?

5 Do any projects benefit from volunteer tourists in the destination? Who is handling this? Could it be developed or strengthened?

2.7 Collateral Benefit from Tourism Investment and Activity

This is about the benefits that poor communities can gain incidentally from the presence of tourism in the destination, rather than as a result of the channelling of tourism spending achieved through the other mechanisms.

It includes:

- spin off benefits from investments made primarily to support tourism development and which would not have been made were it not for that reason;

- general advantages gained from the ongoing operation of tourism.

It relates to activities and investments made by either the public or private sectors. In the private sector context, there are overlaps with mechanisms 4 and 6, which relate to investments and actions knowingly made in the sense of joint venture or philanthropy. With this mechanism 7, the process and benefits are more coincidental.

The benefits arising may be economic, socio/cultural or environmental. The gaining of net benefit can involve reducing negative impacts from tourism as well as strengthening positive ones.

---

39   From presentation at Travelers' Philanthropy Conference, Arusha, Tanzania 2008.

Examples of collateral benefits from infrastructure development and maintenance associated with tourism include:

- access – new roads and bridges, transport provision, telecommunications;

- resources – water supply, energy supply;

- environment – sewage treatment, improved overall maintenance.

Examples of collateral benefits arising from the presence of tourism include:

- cultural – cross-cultural contact, local pride, cultural strengthening;

- social – general education levels, provision of skills related to tourism that are transferable to other activities, health and hygiene awareness;

- environmental – environmental awareness, conservation of biodiversity, ecosystems services (watersheds etc.);

- economic – general dynamism in the economy, economic multiplier effects.

Advantages of this mechanism

- Although hard to quantify, the benefits arising from this collateral impact can be substantial.

- The impacts can be long term and are not much affected by short term fluctuations in tourism performance.

- Most of the benefits can reach everyone in a community, not just those involved in tourism.

Enabling conditions

- Tourism-related investment happening in the destination.

- Tourism enterprises involved in providing and maintaining infrastructure and services.

- Poor communities in locations which can benefit from this.

- Engagement of communities in planning decisions.

- Planning control mechanisms that can influence development.

Issues and challenges

- Opportunities may be missed unless anticipated and planned in advance.

- Governance and planning structures may be insufficient to ensure the necessary leverage.

- Some collateral impacts may be negative.

This mechanism can be hard to pin down and evaluate. It can be difficult to distinguish between those investments and benefits that might have happened anyway and those that are clearly as a result of tourism.

Maximising collateral benefits to poor communities from tourism investment presents a number of challenges in terms of planning and implementation. These include:

* anticipating the potential benefit – requiring some participation of community representatives or those who know their needs;

* finding mechanisms for guiding and influencing private sector investors, especially when development control processes may be rudimentary;

* securing funding for investment by the public sector.

The issue of collateral benefit raises the whole question of the balance between positive and negative impacts of tourism on the poor. Negative impacts were discussed broadly in section 1.3 and Annex 1 of this manual and present a wide set of challenges concerning depletion and competition for resources, especially land and water, loss of cultural integrity, damage to social systems, sexual exploitation and the creation of economic disadvantage through rising prices and disruption to traditional livelihoods.

Actions to pursue

▶ Maintain a strategic, integrated approach to tourism planning and development

In order to maximise the chances of reaping these collateral benefits and avoiding negative impacts, tourism development in the destination should be well planned. It should follow the approach to destination management, influenced by a poverty alleviation objective, which was outlined in part 1 of this manual.

A critically important aspect of this process is the drawing together of the various stakeholders in the destination, as set out in section 1.2. In particular, it is very important to engage the various government/local authority functions that relate to the aspects of collateral impact outlined above – especially land use planning, transport, environment, education and health. The involvement of NGOs and community representatives is also very relevant in foreseeing collateral benefit or negative impacts at the planning stage.

▶ Place requirements on new tourism development projects

A very critical moment for achieving collateral benefits and avoiding negative impacts is at the point when individual tourism developments are being proposed, designed and implemented. Opportunities to influence tourism development and operations and make them pro-poor when the granting of a concession or lease is required have been discussed elsewhere. However, it may be possible to exert influence more widely through general planning and development control processes. This will depend on the legislative basis for development control in the country concerned and the effectiveness of its implementation. Other leverage mechanisms could also be employed.

Relevant actions include:

* Ensuring effective local consultation around any development proposal.

* Requiring Environmental and Social Impact Assessments (ESIA) for all significant tourism development projects. These assessments should pay particular attention to forecasts of resource use, such as water, and impacts on communities.

* Placing requirements on developers to include certain community-benefiting elements in their plans and investments, such as access roads, water schemes etc. – as a form of 'planning gain'.

* Influencing banks, international donors and other funding agencies to link any financial offers to such provisions.

Box 31   Examples of collateral tourism benefit from tourism development

Barra Resorts, Inhambane, Mozambique[40] constructed the Flamingo Bay Water Lodge in 2003. As part of this project, the company built a 200 meter pedestrian bridge in the local village of Ngovene. The bridge was built in collaboration with the local community. The bridge crosses tidal mangrove and swamp land, shortening the distance to the local school and clinic for the community by over three kilometres. In the past many young children were unable to attend school due to the long distances needed to walk. It is now possible for people to get to the clinic all hours of the day in case of emergencies.

The 15 km dirt road that connects to Barra Lodge, Flamingo Bay Lodge and dozens of other tourism establishments needs regular maintenance, which the City Council fails to accomplish. Barra Resorts use their maintenance apparatus and resources to look after the road which benefits hundreds of people each day (other investors included).

Punta Islita Hotel, Costa Rica[41] was built in 1990. At that time the local communities lacked basic services. The infrastructure required to develop the hotel has also benefited the local community. Access roads have been built, together with four bridges, six fords, a handrail crossing of the Corozalito River, a landing strip and telecommunications towers. The local population has also been supplied with drinking water.

▶ **Make investments in infrastructure and environmental management as components of investing in tourism**

As well as placing requirements on developers, governments, local authorities or other agencies should themselves be proactive in making investments that support tourism but also deliver collateral community benefits. Provided they are stimulated or justified by tourism arguments, such investments could be regarded as being part of the overall beneficial impact of tourism on poverty alleviation.

These investments could be made:

- In advance of tourism development and as a way of stimulating private investment – e.g. new road access to a national park improving also the access for neighbouring communities.

- As an integral part of a new tourism project – e.g. a walking trail that is the basis of a new visitor experience but at the same time improves access to certain communities.

- In order to improve the quality of the visitor experience (and hence long term viability) as well as improving amenity for local communities – e.g. rubbish clean ups and investment in garbage disposal plant.

These investments or actions could involve the public sector working alone or in partnership with private developers and/or local communities, with or without external funding support. In all situations, community consultation and engagement and proper environmental and social impact assessments should be undertaken as identified above.

▶ **Reduce negative environmental and social impacts of existing tourism**

Although this mechanism is about bringing positive collateral benefits to poor communities from tourism, there may be some situations where actions which are focussed on eliminating or reducing existing negative collateral impacts from tourism should be taken as a priority. This could be regarded as raising net collateral benefit.

---

40   Case study from SNV Mozambique with input from Barra Lodge.
41   World Tourism Organization, 2003.

The extent and type of any negative impacts should have been revealed during the analysis outlined in part 1. The actions outlined in this manual will serve to address some of the possible negative economic and social issues, such as poor conditions of employment. However, attention should be paid to other negative social, cultural and environmental impacts identified earlier in this section.

The right conditions to start to address the issues can be put in place through the stakeholder engagement and planning processes outlined in part 1. The tourism strategy and action plan for the destination, covered in section 1.6, should include management actions to address the main negative impacts.

It is beyond the scope of this manual to provide detail of relevant actions here. However, two important lines of approach are:

- **To influence private sector enterprises to change their practices.** This could include, for example, reducing water and energy use, improving sewerage treatment, and maintaining good relations with neighbouring communities so that they are aware of any conflicts that may arise. Various tools to influence the private sector were listed in section 1.7.

- **To undertake relevant public initiatives and investment that may help reduce impact.** Examples include improving water and sewerage infrastructure, strengthening environmental maintenance, improving security and taking measures to identify and tackle sexual exploitation.[42]

As has been mentioned above, joint action by the public and private sectors working together can be most effective.

▶ Encourage and facilitate wider community awareness, education etc alongside tourism projects

Many of the intangible collateral benefits arising from the presence of tourism that were listed at the start of this section, such as cultural and environmental awareness, education and skills levels, and overall dynamic effects on the economy, will arise naturally from tourism activity. Some will be stimulated through the various actions associated with the other six mechanisms.

In order to strengthen the chances of poor communities seeing these wider benefits, a particular emphasis should be placed on actions which involve the poor in training and capacity building, learning and skills exchange through joint ventures with private operators, and positive interaction with visitors.

2.7 Considering the collateral benefit mechanism

1 Can you think of situations in your destination where tourism development has led to the provision and/or maintenance of infrastructure and environments that has benefited poor communities?

2 What measures do you think could be taken to control and influence tourism development so that:

– It does not damage the resources of poor communities?

– Developers are made to provide more beneficial infrastructure?

3 Could the government or local authorities do more to make investments that will benefit both tourism and local communities? What are the barriers?

4 Do you believe you have fully identified any negative impacts of tourism on poor communities in your destination that could be exacerbating their poverty? Are actions to address these contained in your action plan?

5 Can you identify any wider social, cultural and environmental benefits stemming from tourism that can help the poor now or in the long term? Is enough being done to stimulate such benefits?

---

42 More information on this can be found in a case study of Costa Rica in World Tourism Organisation, 2009 and through the ECPAT campaign website (www.ecpat.net) (1-11-2009).

Part 3

Assessment –
Monitoring and Evaluation of Impact

The steps and processes outlined in this manual have a primary aim – to alleviate poverty through tourism. For this to be meaningful and continued over time, it is essential to have some way of knowing whether the actions taken have helped towards achieving the aim. This final part of the manual, although short, is therefore as important as the other parts.

There are two sections.

- The first looks at principles and planning of monitoring and evaluation (M & E) and the selection of indicators.

- The second looks in more detail at some measurement processes and the handling of results.

3.1 Planning Monitoring and Evaluation

For monitoring to be successful it needs not only to be well executed but also well planned. This section provides guidance on what to bear in mind when planning and developing a monitoring and evaluation process and the various kinds of indicator that can be selected as a basis for identifying and measuring change and impact.

3.1.1 Integrating M & E into Destination Planning and Actions

Unfortunately, many stakeholders (government, NGOs, partnerships or individuals) responsible for tourism and sustainable development often regard monitoring and evaluation as an add-on to their work, even though they may pay lip service to its importance. As such it can often be squeezed or forgotten in the face of limited time and resources.

By contrast, good practice dictates that monitoring and evaluation should:

- Be fully integrated into the destination planning and management process.

- Be considered and designed from the beginning rather than at the end.

- Influence the choice of interventions not just their assessment. Actions which cannot be monitored should be reconsidered.

- Be given high priority in the allocation of budgets and human resources.

- Involve measurement at different stages, including gathering of baseline data before the strategy and actions are implemented in order to measure change.

The different stages of destination analysis and planning outlined in part 1 of this manual indicated various points where measurement was necessary, for example with respect to policy context (1.1), poverty levels (1.3), the current contribution of tourism to poverty alleviation (1.4), and market trends (1.5). Monitoring and evaluation should be designed to check on the implementation of the strategy and the action plan and the results achieved (1.6). Individual actions, incorporating the different mechanisms outlined in part 2, should be subjected to monitoring and evaluation.

Monitoring activity should clearly seek to measure results related to the pro-poor impact of tourism. However, this should be integrated within the wider monitoring of all aspects of tourism's performance and sustainability.

Monitoring and evaluation can be seen as a cyclical process involving various stages. These have been described[1] as:

1.   plan the monitoring;

2.   identify key issues to monitor;

3.   develop indicators;

4.   collect data;

5.   evaluate results;

6.   plan the response;

7.   communicate the results;

8.   review and adapt.

Stage One needs to look forward to all the subsequent stages and plan for them. Further information relating to the different stages is provided below and in section 3.2.

A number of questions should be addressed when planning and designing a monitoring and evaluation process.[2] These include:

- What is it seeking to achieve – why is it needed?

- How will the results be communicated and used, and by whom?

- What do we really need to know – and what indicators can we use?

- Who will actually undertake the monitoring?

- How will it be done – in particular, what data is needed and how will it be gathered?

Note that in the above list the purpose and results come first. It is very important not to plan to gather data before their use is fully understood, otherwise much energy can be wasted.

Many stakeholders can, and should, be involved in monitoring and evaluation. In order to win support and to focus effort, it should be seen as a key priority of the DM (destination management) group, which should be well placed to provide the necessary coordination.

3.1.2 Agreeing the Purpose of Monitoring

Some of the main reasons why it is important to spend time and resources on monitoring are listed below. Others could be added to the list, some of which may relate to the particular circumstances of the destination.

- To determine the extent to which the aims and objectives of tourism policy have been achieved.

- To underpin the poverty aim – securing political interest by demonstrating the contribution of tourism to poverty alleviation and influencing future policy.

- To help set future targets and make them realistic.

---

1   Twining-Ward, 2007.

2   A more detailed coverage of M & E concepts and requirements is contained in Kruk et al., 2007, which also refers to various models.

- To determine what actions work and what do not – identifying good practice and helping shape future interventions.

- To assess what type of interventions have the highest return on investment.

- To meet the needs of supporting bodies, such as funding agencies, at the outset by demonstrating that actions are results focussed and subsequently by providing evidence of the impact of their support.

- To maintain the interest of stakeholders – through their participation in monitoring and through the provision of results and feedback to them.

- To help beneficiaries reflect on their situation and needs.

3.1.3 Following Some Basic Principles of Monitoring

Some key words and related justification to keep in mind when planning and undertaking monitoring are shown in table 7 below.

These principles have been provided specially for this manual, but they are relevant to most monitoring situations. They relate largely to the design and process of monitoring and have a bearing on who should be involved and their commitment.

Table 7   Principles of monitoring

Achievable	Keep it simple. It is better to focus on a few things that can be measured than to set up an ambitious programme that cannot be carried out properly.
Efficient	Processes must be designed to be efficient and cost effective.
Justifiable	Avoid spending too much time and money on monitoring at the expense of actually taking action.
Meaningful	Results should provide a good picture of what has been happening and help to guide future actions. For this reason, monitoring should be designed so that the full story and implications are well understood. This can be helped by including qualitative as well as quantitative measures, probing reasons for results and enabling people to provide feedback.
Reliable	The results of monitoring should enable robust conclusions to be drawn. Thus results should be unbiased and based on sufficient volumes of data (e.g. sample size in surveys). The causes of change should be investigated so that the extent to which impacts can be attributed to specific interventions can be determined.
Balanced	Positive and negative impacts should be investigated, to show overall net effects.
Participatory	All sorts of stakeholders should be involved in the process. Local communities should have a say in what indicators to use. Participation helps to instil a sense of ownership in the results.
Committing	The various stakeholders involved in interventions and actions, both public and private sector, should commit themselves to gathering data and providing information on results as a condition of their participation.
Sensitive	Some forms of monitoring can be intrusive, which can lead to upset and bias. For example, asking women about levels of income can be insensitive in certain societies – alternative questions could be used, such as ability to buy food.
Replicable	In order to keep track of change over a number of years, monitoring processes should be designed so that they can be repeated in the same way.
Transparent	All stakeholders should be kept aware of monitoring and the processes and results should be made clear and be available for scrutiny.

3.1.4 Selecting Indicators

An important early stage in the monitoring and evaluation process is the identification of possible indicators of the impact of tourism on poverty and the selection of those which are most relevant and practical to use to demonstrate change and impact.

The UNWTO has defined sustainable tourism indicators as 'information sets which are formally selected to be used on a regular basis to measure changes that are of importance for tourism development or management'.[3]

Indicators are normally seen as short written statements which call for a measurement – this may be an absolute figure (the number or amount of something) a relative figure (the percentage of something or a comparative ratio) or a simply a yes/no statement (the presence or absence of something).

As indicators have to be precise, unambiguous and measurable, the process of describing them and selecting which ones to use can be very helpful in sharpening up objectives and actions and defining targets. It is valuable if this exercise can involve the main stakeholders working together as it helps to focus minds individually and collectively. The choice of indicators needs to reflect the main issues and priorities which in turn are addressed in the destination's strategy and actions.

Box 32 Sustainable tourism indicator workshops[4]

Over a fifteen year period UNWTO has worked with many destinations to help them understand the concept and application of sustainability indicators in the planning and management of destinations. One approach has been to facilitate training workshops lasting two to three days for 20 to 30 stakeholders, including representatives of government, local authorities, NGOs and private sector interests. The workshops related to environmental, social and economic sustainability as a whole but poverty alleviation was nearly always addressed as a key topic within them. Workshops have been held in Africa, Asia, Latin America and Europe in destinations selected for the sustainability challenges they represented but also where there was local interest and commitment to make improvements.

The workshops followed a set pattern which evolved over time and was also adjusted to meet local circumstances. In addition to technical presentations on the use of indicators, key interactive stages have included:

- A brief overview of tourism in the destination, with a participatory exercise to identify and list the main stakeholder bodies.

- A short field exercise where participants were asked to visit selected sites and interview small numbers of tourists, businesses and local residents in order to obtain a feel for sustainability issues as well as to learn the value and challenges of practical surveys.

- Working group sessions where participants brainstormed sustainability issues and then prioritised them through a voting system.

- A second round of debate within the groups to propose possible indicators relating to the issues and then reduce them to a short list. Indicators were scrutinised for relevance and feasibility.

- Detailed discussions about the short-listed indicators in order to identify possible data sources and monitoring processes. Indicators that were subsequently considered impractical at this stage could be set aside and others reconsidered.

- Concluding discussions relating issues, indicators, monitoring and actions.

---

3   World Tourism Organization, 2004.

4   Based on UNWTO internal reports.

> Although the workshops threw up many valuable insights about the destinations concerned, they were seen primarily as training and capacity building exercises on the importance of monitoring and the use of indicators, rather than as attempts at actual destination planning, since the latter requires a far more detailed and comprehensive process.

Three types of indicator are useful as the basis for measuring the impact of tourism on poverty.

- **Performance indicators.** These are quantitative indicators of the state of tourism, the economy and poverty. Examples include tourist volumes, level of earnings, number of poor people employed.

- **Process indicators.** These indicate relevant policy conditions or participation in an intervention. They can be used to reveal good governance and progress with planned actions. Examples include the presence/absence of a minimum wage policy or the percentage of enterprises committed to sourcing food from the poor.

- **Perception indicators.** These show the proportion of stakeholders holding certain opinions. An example is the percentage of residents in a community believing their livelihood has improved as a result of tourism. These are sometimes referred to as opinion indicators.

Baseline indicators, which may be made up of all the above three types of indicator, describe the situation at a given time, against which change can be measured.

The selection of indicators should reflect the principles of monitoring listed earlier.

Good indicators are easy to measure and understand. They should meet criteria of relevance, availability, credibility, clarity and comparability. It is sensible to start with a small set and then build this up as necessary.

The indicators that are selected should clearly be relevant to the poverty alleviation objectives and targets in the destination as a whole. Examples of possible indicators in this respect are given later in section 3.2.3. More specific indicators should also be designed to relate to interventions made. A set of possible indicators relating to each of the seven mechanisms described in part 2 was prepared by UNWTO in 2008 and is presented in Annex 4. These are divided into (A) Performance (benefits from tourism), (B) Process (enabling environment and support activities) and (C) Perception (stakeholder satisfaction) indicators.

3.1 Considering the role of monitoring/evaluation and the use of indicators

1 How much monitoring and evaluation of tourism is already happening in your destination and does this include impact on poverty?

2 Consider the purposes of monitoring. Which do you think are the most important in your destination?

3 How easy do you think it will be to find resources for monitoring and to commit others to participate in it? Who should be involved?

4 Looking back at your poverty targets (section 1.3), strategic priorities (1.6) and actions (part 2), what kinds of indicator do you feel relate best to them?

3.2 Measuring Change and the Effectiveness of Actions

This section looks in more detail at the kinds of measurement and monitoring that can be undertaken, considering generic measurement of pro-poor tourism performance in the destination and specific assessment of interventions. It also looks at processes for evaluating and communicating the results.

3.2.1 Using Data Sources and Surveys

A range of different sources and processes can be used to gather data on poverty, tourism and the relationship between them. Their availability and practicability will vary significantly between destinations.

- **Economic performance and poverty records**

  Basic data on economic performance may be recorded for the destination itself or for a larger area (e.g. region) that contains the destination. This may include poverty-related data as described in section 1.3, including economic output, income levels, employment levels, poverty-line statistics and other welfare data.

- **Data on tourism volume, value and performance**

  Data on visitor arrivals, origins and length of stay is quite often available from official sources but may not relate precisely to the destination. Performance data, such as occupancy levels of registered hotels or admission to attractions, may be available. Quality of data may vary and collection methods should be scrutinised.

- **Audits of tourism products and facilities**

  Supply side measurement can involve systematic counts of numbers of tourism products and facilities (hotels, service providers etc.) including details of size/capacity and quality grade (if available). Enterprise closures and new developments should be noted.

- **Enterprise surveys**

  These are hugely important in monitoring tourism and pro-poor engagement and impact. DM groups should give high priority to encouraging individual enterprises to commit to answering regular, preferably annual, surveys. These should cover economic performance, employment levels, pay, recruitment activity, procurement and sources, issues and barriers and relevant actions taken. More detail on relevant questions is provided in Annex 2. Associated surveys of employees can be very helpful in monitoring attitudes and impacts. Surveys should also cover enterprises down the supply chain.

- **Visitor surveys**

  These are important for identifying market profiles and response, spending patterns, factors influencing spending, interest in supporting poor communities and reaction to certain interventions. Again, Annex 2 provides more details concerning survey processes and coverage of questions. Visitor surveys can also be used to monitor change over time provided they are based on sizeable samples and consistent survey conditions.

- **Household surveys**

  These can be very valuable in monitoring and evaluating outcomes and impacts as they provide direct access to the poor. Sample surveys should seek to reach households that are identified targets for poverty alleviation (by geography, type etc.). The surveys are likely to require direct interviews. Questions should cover household make-up and general measures of poverty and wellbeing, including income levels, expenditure, needs and aspirations, and then seek to identify the contribution of tourism related activity to this, including the impact of specific interventions where relevant. Barriers and opportunities should be discussed, and actual and perceived negative as well as positive impacts of tourism should be investigated. Use of perception indicators can be very appropriate here.

- **Objective records, physical assessment and observation**

  Monitoring can involve systematic recording of activity over time, such as records of events, meetings etc, and observation of investments and development occurring. Photographic records can be helpful here.

- **Stakeholder discussions and feedback**

  Qualitative monitoring through consultation and feedback can be very valuable, especially where it can back up more quantitative measurement. It can be essential in understanding the causes of change.

Monitoring could entail simply selecting one or more of the above sources and processes and using them to make measurements against indicators, selected as described in section 3.1. However, it may be more effective to use them more systematically as described below.

3.2.2 Considering Both the Big Picture and Specific Interventions

Monitoring and evaluating the impacts of tourism on poverty in a destination can be tackled through three different types of measurement:

- **Using broad measures of poverty.** This involves simply looking for change using the basic statistics collected in most destinations, such as levels of GDP per head, numbers of people below the poverty line etc. They were described in section 1.3 of this manual.

- **Tracking the pro-poor impact of the tourism sector.** This is a much more focussed approach and entails making estimates of the extent to which the poor are engaged in the tourism value chain and the benefits they are getting from it.

- **Evaluating the results of interventions.** This involves looking at specific actions taken and directing monitoring at understanding the consequences for the poor that can be attributed to the intervention.

It has been suggested[5] that it is unrealistic to expect that the first of these can really show the impact of tourism as there will always be many other factors at play.

The other two types of measurement are both equally valuable however. One provides the big picture, to inform overall policy and direction. The other is required to provide feedback to stakeholders to guide the design of future interventions. Both will be described in more detail below.

3.2.3 Measuring Overall Change in the Pro-poor Performance of Tourism

Monitoring the big picture of pro-poor impact of tourism in the destination can be based on the kind of approach to tourism value chain analysis that was set out in section 1.4 of this manual. The application of this analysis to monitoring and evaluation of impacts has been addressed in work undertaken for SNV Asia and other partners[6] and the summary that follows is based partly on this.

The monitoring should be based around the target beneficiaries identified in the destination and they should be kept in mind throughout. This was discussed in section 1.3 and should be reflected in the tourism strategy (1.6).

Although there will be a considerable variation between destinations, there are a number of key aspects of poverty, as may be influenced by tourism, that are likely to be of particular interest in most destinations. These are listed in table 8, together with suggestions of possible indicators and data sources to use in monitoring.

5   Goodwin, 2006b

6   Ashley and Mitchell, 2008.

Table 8   Key changes to measure

Change in	Possible indicators	Data sources
The numbers of poor people/households participating in the tourism value chain and reasons for the change.	• Total poor employed in tourism enterprises or engaged in supply chain. • Number of poor recruited/ entering employment in specific period or joining supply chains. • Growth in tourism volume and spend. • Number of new enterprises established or expanded.	• Value Chain Analysis exercise as described in section 1.4. • Enterprise survey. • Tourism volume/value data in destination. • Visitor survey. • Enterprise inventory.
The types of poor people involved – do they include certain target beneficiaries?	• % women participating/ joining. • % ethnic groups/minorities. • % identified needy/ target groups.	• Enterprise survey. • Household survey (focus on target groups).
Their geographical clustering or spread - reflecting any spatial priorities.	• Employment levels in target communities. • Location of new jobs by area.	• Enterprise inventory by area. • Enterprises survey. • Supply chain mapping. • Household surveys in target communities.
Levels of increase (or decrease) in income of the participating poor and reasons for this.	• % of those participating in income reporting rise in income. • Increase in hours, production levels etc. • % upgrading jobs.	• Enterprise survey (including workers and producers in supply chain). • Household survey.
The overall effect on the wellbeing of the households involved.	• Level of household income from tourism c.f. total/other sectors. • % households satisfied with tourism income and level of perceived importance to them. • % households making investments to benefit their wellbeing. • Observable investment in communities.	• Enterprise survey (including workers and producers in supply chain). • Household survey. • Systematic physical observation.
Other economic, social and environmental conditions.	• Satisfaction/ dissatisfaction in communities with aspects of tourism (perception indicators). • Indicators of resource use/ availability: water, land etc. • % poor people participating in education and training.	• Household survey. • Local land use and environment records. • Systematic physical observation. • Recorded participation in training etc.

In order to place these changes in context, monitoring should also cover:

• Overall changes in tourism performance in the destination – tourist arrivals, length of stay, market trends.

• Changes in policies, attitudes etc. (including a summary of known interventions) creating an enabling environment for pro-poor tourism. This could use process and perception indicators.

In addition to monitoring actual change, the process should also probe and reveal causes and effects – asking 'how?' and 'why?' questions.

The monitoring will require an approach to data gathering similar to that required for the Value Chain Analysis (Pro-poor impact) outlined in section 1.4. Re-running of the VCA periodically would be a very valuable monitoring procedure. However, in order to look at the degree and impact of change, more detail will be required about the implicated poor and their individual circumstances and livelihoods.

The surveys involved were outlined in Annex 2, which includes an indication of questions to ask. They include a number of processes described above, including:

- Discussions with key players.

- Auditing and observation of enterprises (type, size, location – closures and start-ups).

- Enterprise surveys (including any new enterprises formed) to cover change in performance and the participation of the poor, and actions taken.

In addition, in order to evaluate actual impacts, household surveys should be used in the monitoring, based on selected samples.

Surveys should be designed so that they are relatively straightforward to carry out, based around a small number of clear indicators. In order to get a reasonably robust indication of the extent of change, the sampling methods and questions should be kept as constant as possible.

A decision should be taken at the outset on whether this monitoring should attempt to form a broad picture of change across the destination or focus on particular aspects of tourism – e.g. a particular area, type of product or type of enterprise. These may be of interest because of their strategic importance, potential for growth or assumed relevance to certain policy targets. They may also relate to known interventions. A more focussed approach will be less time consuming and provide more robust results.

Irrespective of the degree of focus in the design, the results may also be considered at different levels:

- Across the destination as a whole.

- Within certain types or clusters of enterprise – relating to types of product.

- For households of different size, type and location.

3.2.4 Measuring the Results of Interventions

The results of interventions may be shown up from the broad-picture monitoring described above. However, a more direct process is to track this through from the intervention itself. This is more likely to ensure that changes measured are actually due to the intervention rather than as a result of other external and internal circumstances.

It is common to refer to four stages associated with the implementation and consequences of an intervention: inputs, outputs, outcomes and impacts. Each of these can be measured.

- **Inputs –** *The resources required to make the intervention – money, time, skills etc.*

  Inputs can be monitored easily by keeping accurate records, including accounts and time sheets.

  It is necessary to monitor inputs if a **return on investment** is to be calculated or estimated. This is a ratio of inputs (costs) to outcomes or impacts, preferably in the form of monetary values but it can also be expressed in other ways. It is a measure increasingly required by funding agencies and used in business planning.

- **Outputs –** *The specific actions taken or delivered – such as workshops held and the number of participants.*

  As with inputs, outputs can be monitored through diligent record keeping. It is important to record aspects relevant to the poverty aim– e.g. number of women participating. Verification can occur through minutes, records of attendance, reports and pictures.

- **Outcomes** – *The consequence of the outputs – such as a number of SMEs preparing their own business plans as a result of the workshops.*

  This requires monitoring to identify and measure the capacities gained and initiatives emerging as a result of an intervention. It may involve probing the opinions, actions and performance of people engaged and targeted in the intervention, through retrospective surveys and discussion.

  Outcomes may also relate to tourists, such as an increase in numbers visiting or spend per head. Visitor surveys can be used here, with questions which seek to find out whether the visitor response has been stimulated by the intervention.

- **Impacts** – *The resultant changes that occur – such as an increase in household income.*

  Impacts are hardest to measure but are critical in terms of assessing poverty alleviation. One problem is that impacts may take a long time to materialise after the intervention ceased.

  Monitoring the impacts of interventions could take the following approaches:

  - direct recording of any known results, such as specific new jobs created;

  - estimating visitor spending generated, through visitor numbers and spend per head, and using a combination of visitor and enterprise surveys to trace how much of this may have reached poor households;

  - further probing of participants and beneficiaries of interventions, as with outcomes but taking this to a next level to determine impacts on income, livelihood etc. Knowledge of household structure would help in estimating total number of people benefiting from new income;

  - considering the use of control groups (households not possibly reached by the intervention) to see how their livelihoods have changed over a comparable period.

Interventions may relate to the mechanisms described in part 2 of the manual. It is helpful to consider how the use of monitoring and surveys may relate to specific indicators referred to in section 3.1 and listed in Annex 4.

Box 33 Practical monitoring leading to actionable conclusions[7]

The development of the Nabji-Korphu trek in Bhutan, described in box 4 in section 1.3, provides a good example of straightforward monitoring of an intervention in a way that revealed helpful and practical results. Prior to the initiative starting, the economic, social and environmental conditions of the communities were assessed and this provided some baseline data to enable progress to be measured. After the project had run for one year, a number of surveys were carried out to measure outcomes and impacts. These included:

A household survey. This involved an interviewer-administered questionnaire of 114 randomly selected households. Initial village meetings were convened with the household representatives to explain the survey. The number of households selected in each village was related to the village size. Meetings and interviews were conducted in the evenings in order not to disturb daily work. Direct participation in the trek project (such as providing portering services) as well as perceived indirect benefits were recorded. Questions probed levels of income earned, how this was spent, female participation, effect on traditional work, attitude to visitors, perceptions of social and environmental impacts, barriers to participation, and interest in further enterprise development.

A visitor survey. This was based on a self-completion questionnaire distributed by the tour operators. 55% of tourists using the trail completed the questionnaire and returned it to the operator in a sealed envelope. Questions covered profile data (age, origin, party type, education, previous visit patterns), length of stay, sources of information, satisfaction and suggestions for improvement, prices paid and perceptions of value for money.

---

7   Dorji, 2007.

Discussions and feedback with tour operators. This covered impressions of the product and recommendations for improvement and strengthening income-earning activities for poor communities, including guiding, handicrafts, provision of local produce, camping fees, cultural activities, and issues with gratuities.

The monitoring and evaluation was enshrined in a comprehensive report which contained over 30 practical recommendations for the different stakeholders involved with the project.

3.2.5 Interpreting, Disseminating and Using the Findings

There is little point in monitoring unless the results are acted upon. The evaluation stages and what follows from them are equally as important as the monitoring itself.

As well as coordinating the monitoring, the destination management (DM) group, (which brings together the public and private sectors, NGOs and community representatives) should also take responsibility for the results. Three further stages can be identified and sufficient time should be allowed for each.

Analysing and interpreting the results

The monitoring will provide a set of results for selected indicators. As described above, these may provide a full picture or relate to specific interventions, will variously cover performance, process and perceptions, and may relate to inputs, outputs, outcomes and impacts.

It will now be necessary to decide what the results mean. Is the result good, moderate or bad? This will require some comparison with:

- A previous situation – what has been the direction and rate of change?

- Desired results – what was expected and were some targets set?

- Performance elsewhere – are there comparable results from other destinations?

Time should be spent in considering the reasons for the results. There should be various clues from the feedback obtained from the monitoring. Where highly unexpected results are found, it is sensible to double check the monitoring process to see if the explanation lies in the methodology or its execution.

Communicating the results to stakeholders

It was suggested in section 3.1 that a commitment to monitoring, or at least providing information, should be a condition of stakeholder participation in actions. A matching commitment should be to provide these stakeholders with the results.

Some good practice to follow includes:

- If appropriate, hold a meeting to present the results and discuss conclusions, implications and action.

- Highlight the main results as too much information can be off-putting, but make all data available on request in the interests of transparency.

- Use simple communication techniques, such as graphs, colour coding, smiles/ frowns, etc.

- Adopt a cycle of annual reporting, which is a good discipline for monitoring and means that stakeholders come to expect and ask for results.

Reviewing and adapting the strategy, actions and monitoring

The results of monitoring and evaluation should guide future policies and actions. This may vary from simple adjustments to short term actions to more far reaching and long term changes.

In particular, the DM group should make sure that the lessons from the monitoring are taken on board in the next review and revision of the destination's tourism strategy and action plan for which it is responsible.

Lessons should also be learnt for the monitoring process itself, which should be regularly adapted to make it more efficient and focussed while winning support for it and ensuring its future.

3.2 Considering monitoring processes and the use of results

1 Think about the data sources in your area. How relevant and robust is the information they might provide?

2 How easy would it be for you to conduct enterprise, visitor and household surveys? Do you have the resources for this? Could different stakeholders help?

3 Think about the need to understand the big picture – i.e. whether tourism has provided more benefits for the poor over time – as against the evaluation of specific interventions. Which is the most important for you?

4 How will you use and communicate the results of monitoring and evaluation? Will you use what you learn from the experience and share it with others or put the information on a shelf?

Bibliography and Websites

Ashley, C. (2006), *How Can Governments Boost the Local Economic Impacts of Tourism?*, SNV and ODI, The Hague/London.

Ashley, C. (2006b), *Participation by the Poor in Luang Prabang tourism Economy: Current Earnings and Opportunities for Expansion*, ODI Working Paper 273, ODI, London.

Ashley, C. (2006c), *Luang Prabang Tourism and Opportunities for the Poor*, ODI and SNV, Vientiane.

Ashley, C., Boyd, C. and Goodwin, H. (2000), 'Pro-poor Tourism: Putting Poverty at the Heart of the Tourism Agenda, *Natural Resource Perspectives*, No 51.

Ashley, C., Goodwin, H., McNab, D., Scott, M. and Chaves, L. (2006), *Making Tourism Count for the Local Economy in the Caribbean*, Pro-poor Tourism Partnership and Caribbean Tourism Organisation, Barbados.

Ashley, C. and Goodwin, H. (2007), 'Pro-poor Tourism' – What's Gone Right and What's Gone Wrong?, *Opinion 80*, ODI, London.

Ashley, C. and Haysom, G. (2008), 'The Development Impacts of Tourism Supply Chains: Increasing Impact on Poverty and Decreasing Our Ignorance', in: Spenceley, A. (ed.), *Responsible Tourism: Critical Issues for Conservation and Development*, Earthscan, London.

Ashley, C. and Haysom, G. (2009), *Bringing Local Entrepreneurs into the Supply Chain: The Experience of Spier*, ODI Project Briefing 20, ODI, London.

Ashley, C. and Mitchell, J. (2008), *Doing the Right Thing Approximately not the Wrong Thing Precisely: Challenges of Monitoring Impacts of Pro-poor Interventions in Tourism Value Chains*, ODI Working Paper 291, SNV, IFC, ODI, London.

Ashley, C. and Roe, D. (1998), *Enhancing Community Involvement in Wildlife Tourism: Issues and Challenges*, IIED Wildlife and Development Series, No. 11.

Bah, A. and Goodwin, H. (2003), *Improving Access for the Informal Sector to Tourism in The Gambia*, Pro-Poor Tourism Partnership, Working Paper No.15, London.

Beddoe, C. (2004), *Labour Standards, Social Responsibility and Tourism*, Tourism Concern, London.

Deen, M. (2001), *Willingness to Pay Study, for the Fee System in Sa Pa*, SNV Viet Nam, CCIST Sa Pa, and IUCN Viet Nam, Hanoi.

Department for International Development, UK (2002), *Tools for Development: A Handbook for Those Engaged in Development Activity*, Version 15, DFID, London.

Dixey, L. M. (2005), *Inventory and Analysis of Community-based Tourism in Zambia. Production, Finance and Technology*, USAID Private Sector Development, Lusaka.

Dorji, P. (2007), *Nabji-Korphu Trek: The Piloted Community-Based Nature Tourism Project in Bhutan*, Department of Tourism, Royal Government of Bhutan.

Goodwin, H. (2006), *Handouts and Summary Report from UNWTO Seminar on Tourism and Poverty Alleviation*, Arusha, Tanzania, UNWTO, Madrid.

Goodwin, H. (2006b), *Measuring and Reporting the Impact of Tourism on Poverty*, paper delivered at the School of Management, University of Surrey, June 2006.

Gujadhur, T. (2008), *Pro-poor Sustainable Tourism in Luang Parbang, Lao PDR: A Value Chain Analysis of Rural Excursions*, SNV Lao, Vientiane.

Ham, S (2009), *The Psychology of Giving,* University of Idaho.

Kruk, E., Hummel, J. and Banskota, K. (2007), *Facilitating Sustainable Mountain Tourism,* Volume 1 (Resource Book) and Volume 2 (Toolkit), International Centre for Integrated Mountain Development, Kathmandu, 2007.

Lyons, K. and Wearing, S. (2008), *Journeys of Discovery in Volunteer Tourism: International Case Study Perspectives,* CABI, Wallingford.

Mann, S. (2005), *Development Through Tourism: The World Bank's Role,* World Bank, Washington DC.

Mitchell, J., Keane, J. and Laidlaw, J. (2009), *Making Success Work for the Poor: Package Tourism in Northern Tanzania,* ODI and SNV, London.

Nepal Tourism Board (2008), *Building Nepal's Private Sector Capacity for Sustainable Tourism Operations,* UNEP, SNV Nepal, Nepal Tourism Board.

Pro-Poor Tourism Partnership (2004), *Tourism in Poverty Reduction Strategy Papers (PRSPs),* PPTP Sheet No. 9, PPTP, London.

Pro-Poor Tourism Partnership (2005), *Annual Register 2005,* PPTP, London.

Pro-Poor Tourism Pilots (2004), *Tourism-agricultural Linkages: Boosting Inputs from Local Farmers,* Business Implementation of Pro Poor Tourism: Case Study Brief No.3, PPT in Practice, London.

Ravallion, M. and Chen, S. (2008), *The Developing World is Poorer than We Thought, but no less Successful in the Fight Against Poverty,* World Bank, Washington DC.

Relly, P. (2008), 'Madikwe Game Reserve, South Africa – Investment and Employment', in: Spenceley, A. (ed.) *Responsible Tourism: Critical Issues for Conservation and Development,* Earthscan, London.

Rinzin, C., Vermeulen, W . J. V and Glasbergen, P. (2007), 'Ecotourism as a Mechanism for Sustainable Development: the Case of Bhutan', *in: Environmental Sciences,* 4 (2), pp. 109-125.

Sandbrook, C. (2009), *Bwindi Advanced Market Gardeners' Association (AMAGARA),* Project summary.

Saville, N. (2002), *Sustainable Ecotourism and Eco-enterprise Opportunities in the Gulf of Mannar, Tamil Nadu, India,* M. S. Swaminathan Research Foundation.

Scheyvens, R. (2007), 'Exploring the Tourism-Poverty Nexus', *Current Issues in Tourism,* 10 (2-3), pp. 231-254.

Schipani, S. (2008), *Alleviating Poverty and Protecting Cultural and Natural Heritage through Community-based Ecotourism in Luang Namtha,* UNESCO, Bangkok.

Smith, R. and Henderson, J. (2008), 'Integrated Beach Resorts, Informal Tourism Commerce and the 2004 Tsunami: Laguna Phuket in Thailand', *International Journal of Tourism Research,* 10, pp. 271-282.

SNV Nepal (2004), *Developing Sustainable Communities: A Toolkit for Development Practitioners,* ICIMOD, Kathmandu.

SNV Nepal (2006), *Pro-poor Sustainable Tourism Lessons Learned in Nepal,* SNV, Kathmandu.

Spenceley, A. (2008), *Responsible Tourism: Critical Issues for Conservation and Development,* Earthscan, London.

Spenceley, A. (2008b), 'Local Impacts of Community-based Tourism in Southern Africa', in: Spenceley, A. (ed.), *Responsible Tourism: Critical Issues for Conservation and Development,* Earthscan, London.

Torres, R. and Momson, J. H. (2004), 'Challenges and Potential for Linking Tourism and Agriculture to Achieve Pro-Poor Tourism Objectives', *Progress in Development Studies,* 4 (4): pp. 294-318.

Tourism for Rural Poverty Alleviation Programme (2003), *Mid-term Evaluation Report,* TRPAP, Kathmandu.

Twining-Ward, L. (2007), *A Toolkit for Monitoring and Managing Community-based Tourism,* University of Hawaii and SNV Viet Nam, Hanoi.

United Nations Environment Programme (2008), *Building Nepal's Private Sector Capacity for Sustainable Tourism Operations,* UNEP/Nepal Tourism Board/SNV Nepal, Paris.

Varghese, G. (2008), 'Public-Private Partnerships in South African National Parks: The Rationale, Benefits and Lessons Learned' in: Spenceley, A. (ed.), *Responsible Tourism: Critical Issues for Conservation and Development,* Earthscan, London.

World Bank (2007), *More Than a Pretty Picture: Using Poverty Maps to Design Better Policies and Interventions,* World Bank, Washington DC.

World Tourism Organization (2002), *Tourism and Poverty Alleviation,* UNWTO, Madrid.

World Tourism Organization (2003), *Sustainable Development of Ecotourism: A Compilation of Good Practices in SMEs,* UNWTO, Madrid.

World Tourism Organization (2004), *Indicators of Sustainable Development for Tourism Destinations: A Guidebook,* UNWTO, Madrid.

World Tourism Organization (2004b), *Tourism and Poverty Alleviation: Recommendations for Action,* UNWTO, Madrid.

World Tourism Organization (2005), *Making Tourism More Sustainable: A Guide for Policymakers,* UNWTO and UNEP, Madrid.

World Tourism Organization (2005b), *Tourism, Microfinance and Poverty Alleviation,* UNWTO, Madrid.

World Tourism Organization (2006), *Poverty Alleviation Through Tourism – A Compilation of Good Practices,* UNWTO, Madrid.

World Tourism Organization (2007), *A Practical Guide to Tourism Destination Management,* UNWTO, Madrid.

World Tourism Organization (2010), *Joining Forces – Collaborative Processes for Sustainable and Competitive Tourism,* UNWTO/SNV, Madrid.

World Tourism Organization (undated), *ST-EP Programme: Sustainable Tourism – Eliminating Poverty,* UNWTO, Madrid.

Websites containing helpful information

Overseas Development Institute (ODI): www.odi.org.uk

Information and resource materials on many aspects of sustainable development. Coverage of value chain analysis and other relevant techniques. Many downloadable papers and publications relating to tourism and poverty alleviation.

Pro-poor tourism partnership: www.propoortourism.org.uk

A considerable collection of downloadable papers and publications specifically on pro-poor tourism, including findings from original research, case studies, discussion papers etc. up to 2007.

SNV – Netherlands Development Organisation: www.snvworld.org

Regularly updated information on sustainable development and tourism projects and initiatives. Separate sections on Asia, Latin America, Balkans, East and Southern Africa, West and Central Africa. Pages on sustainable tourism and many free downloadable publications on this subject.

Tourism Concern: www.tourismconcern.org.uk

News items and articles on key social tourism topics, including human rights, labour issues, community relations etc. Various publications, including original research reports, can be ordered.

United Nations Environment Programme (UNEP): www.unep.fr/scp/tourism

Information on various global initiatives promoting sustainable consumption and production, including tourism. Free downloadable studies and policy documents on sustainable tourism with relevance to poverty alleviation.

UNWTO ST-EP Foundation: www.unwtostep.org

Lists and information on tourism and poverty alleviation projects supported by the ST-EP programme, together with news items and current activities.

UNWTO – World Tourism Organization: www.unwto.org

Data on tourism trends and forecasts. Information on markets, projects and upcoming events. Sizeable library of purchasable, downloadable publications on: destination management; sustainable development of tourism; tourism and poverty; heritage tourism; education and training; and many other tourism topics.

World Bank: www.worldbank.org

Information on global trends. Searchable data by country on economic performance, industry sectors and poverty. Many economic and social research publications.

World Travel and Tourism Council: www.wttc.org

Information on tourism industry positions and perspectives. Economic data for the tourism industry. Topic papers. Case studies from Tourism for Tomorrow awards.

List of Figures, Tables and Boxes

List of Acronyms

CBT	Community-based tourism
CBTs	Community-based tourism projects/enterprises
CSR	Corporate social responsibility
DM	Destination management
DMO	Destination management organization
ESIA	Environmental and social impact assessment
GDP	Gross domestic product
M & E	Monitoring and evaluation
MDW	Multiple destination workshop
MFI	Micro-finance institution
NGO	Non-governmental organization
PPEI	Pro-poor employment income
PPI	Pro-poor impact
PPT	Pro-poor tourism
PRSP	Poverty reduction strategy paper
SDW	Single destination workshop
SME	Small or micro enterprise
SNV	Netherlands Development Organization
ST-EP	Sustainable Tourism – Elimination of Poverty
TO	Tour operator
TVC	Tourism value chain
UNWTO	World Tourism Organization
USP	Unique selling proposition
VCA	Value chain analysis

The Livelihoods Approach

Adapted from inputs to UNWTO Seminar on Tourism and Poverty Alleviation,
Arusha, Tanzania, Harol Goodwin, 2006

Livelihood analysis is a methodology which can be used to analyse the contribution that different forms of tourism might make to the livelihoods of the poor or other groups new to tourism. The advantage of livelihood analysis is that it provides a methodology to assess the positive and negative impacts of a particular form of tourism development upon the livelihoods of the poor – this approach ensures that net benefits can be identified and negative impacts mitigated.

The livelihoods approach is a form of systematic analysis that seeks to assess the many issues that affect how the poor put their living together, sustain their families and maximise their security. It goes beyond what is often thought of as 'economic' (earnings) or 'social' (health, culture) impacts. An assessment of tourism's impact on local people depends not only on its direct costs and benefits, such as profits and jobs generated, but also on how:

1   these relate to the various household needs;

2   they affect the other household strategies (supporting or conflicting).

You do not need to be an expert in sustainable livelihoods analysis to be able to gain insights and focus from understanding and using the approach. See the Livelihoods Connect web pages[1] for an introduction to livelihoods approaches and introductory training and learning materials, including Sustainable Livelihoods Analysis guidance sheets and a distance learning guide.

The Livelihoods Framework

First it is important to define what we mean when we talk about livelihoods, as the term can be used in many different ways. Essentially a livelihood is the mix of capabilities, assets, and activities people use to meet their basic needs and support their well-being. The Livelihoods Framework, adopted by the UK Department for International Development (DFID) seeks to understand people's strengths, including their skills and possessions, and how they use these assets to improve the quality of their lives. It views people as having access to five types of asset or capital:

1.   human (skills, ability to work, health);

2.   natural (natural resources, biodiversity, environment);

3.   financial (cash – or equivalent);

4.   social (membership of networks and groups, relationships, norms);

5.   physical (transport, shelter, water and sanitation, energy, communications).

Achieving sustainable livelihoods requires the development of an appropriate balance between these essential assets. The mix and level of these different assets is influenced by external institutions and processes, and determines the livelihood strategies adopted (or choices made to make a living) and their subsequent outcomes (such as more income, or reduced vulnerability).

---

1   http://www.eldis.org/go/topics/dossiers/livelihoods-connect (Accessed 1-11-2009)

The sustainable livelihoods framework

Livelihood assets
Vulnerability context
Shocks
Trends
Seasonality
H
S
N
P
F
Policies, institutions processes
Level of government
Private sector
Laws
Culture
Policies
Institutions
Livelihood strategies
Livelihood outcomes
More income
Increased well-being
Reduced vulnerability
Improved food security
More sustainable use of natural resources
Influence and access
Key
H = Human capital   S = Social capital   F= Financial capital
N = Natural capital   P = Physical capital

There is no single tool or methodology for assessing livelihood impacts. The Sustainable Livelihoods Framework, however, provides a structured way of thinking through the various types of impact that may need to be considered, where they might occur and how they might be manifest. Gaining a full understanding of the impacts of any intervention on poor peoples' livelihoods means not just looking at obvious poverty indicators such as changes in cash income, but also at how other dimensions of well-being – food security, vulnerability, social standing – are affected:

> "All too often the emphasis in development work is on increasing financial capital. While this is important, development practitioners should not lose sight of the need to work with local people to increase their other assets (social, physical, natural and human). These other assets support the accumulation of financial capital. In fact for many resource-poor people, the reality is that they may be unable to increase their financial capital without these assets."

Interventions may have a direct impact on one or more of the five assets available to poor people, or may affect these assets indirectly because of their impact on the external environment (the "vulnerability context" or "policies, institutions and processes" in the above diagram). It is also important to remember that different peoples' livelihoods are constructed in different ways and have different priorities. This means that different individuals, households, or groups are likely to be affected in different ways by the same intervention. Analysis thus has to be undertaken locally in specific places.

Applying Livelihoods Analysis to Tourism

The livelihoods approach is generally, but not exclusively, applied in rural environments. It is relevant in any situation where a defined community is considering engaging with tourism and where this will be one amongst a number of livelihood strategies. The technique is also useful in identifying potential linkages between tourism and other livelihood activities.

Since livelihood strategies differ between households and between men and women, there is no single answer to what will optimise livelihood impact in a community. Some will lose and gain more than others. The results may also vary between adjacent communities – and people working with local communities may want to encourage this in order to create complementary rather than competitive tourism goods and services.

Ashley & Roe (1998)[2] extrapolated from livelihoods analysis at local levels in Namibia combined with research elsewhere, to summarise a range of potential advantages and disadvantages of tourism for livelihoods of poor people in sub-Saharan Africa. See the table below.

Tourism affects	Possible positive impacts tourism can	Possible negative effects tourism can
Other livelihood activities	Complement other activities *eg: if tourism earnings peak in agricultural hungry season; development of transferable skills.*	Conflict with other activities *eg: conflicts with agriculture, if tourism imposes labour demands at busy agricultural seasons and/or results in increased wildlife damage to crops and livestock.*
Capital assets	Build up assets (natural, physical, financial, human, and social) *eg: enhanced physical assets, if earnings are invested in productive capital; enhanced natural capital, if sustainability of natural resource management is improved.*	Erode assets *eg: undermine natural capital if local people excluded from tourism areas lose access to natural resources; erode social capital if conflict over tourism undermines social and reciprocal relations.*
Policy and institutional influences on livelihoods	Enhance residents' power to change and improve the policy/institutional context *eg: if participation in tourism planning and enterprise gives them new status, information and skills to deal with outsiders.*	Exacerbate policy constraints *eg: diminish opportunities if policy–makers divert attention, resources and infra–structure investment to prioritise tourism over other local activities.*
Long-term priorities	'Fit' with people's underlying long–term priorities *eg: to diversify risk, or build buffers against drought, by developing an additional source of income which continues in drought years.*	Create or exacerbate threats to long–term security *eg: physical threats from more aggressive wild animals due to disturbance by tourists. Economic vulnerability due to dependence on volatile tourism.*

As Ashley and Roe point out:

> *"Rural households rarely rely on one activity or source of income. In order to diversify risk and exploit available opportunities they combine [a variety of] income sources, drawing on a range of natural resources, and build up physical, social and human assets for long term security. While tourism can complement their other livelihood activities and priorities, it can also conflict with them. Trade-offs with agriculture are particularly acute, not only due to competition for land, but also due to wildlife damage to agriculture, (elephants eating crops, and predators attacking livestock), and, if the agricultural and tourism seasons coincide, competition for time… The fact that tourism earnings are often unreliable, involve high investment, and a delay before earnings flow, can also conflict with livelihood strategies of poor households to maintain flexibility and minimise risk."*

Seasonality is a particular issue and it is important to consider how tourism will affect harvests and other seasonal work in the destinations. However, this is only an issue if a very large proportion of the economically active population is to be engaged in tourism; and it should be remembered that if people are tempted out of agriculture into tourism it is often for sound economic reasons and at least in part because there are no tariff barriers imposed by the international market countries – particularly Europe and North America.

In Tamil Nadu, Saville[3] found that the fishing season and the tourism season both occurred at the same time and that the community was almost entirely dependent on marine resources, and identified the risk

---

2   Ashley and Roe, 1998.

3   Saville, 2002.

that working in the tourism industry may deplete the household workforce in the season so as to make fishing non-viable. In this case net benefit would be less or potentially negative.

It is easy to overlook the importance of social capital. If tourism development divides communities and increases conflict, such negative impacts have to be considered when assessing net benefit. Social capital may increase or decrease depending upon the way in which the community is engaged in decision making about tourism development. Tourism is often welcomed for valuing local culture, and may lead to a positive revaluation of local culture. Tourism may serve to encourage young people to take a more positive view of their heritage and to engage with it. This engagement may assist in keeping cultures alive and in ameliorating the impacts of urban-drift. However, it may also create problems of commercialisation, acculturation, dissatisfaction and alienation.

Whilst tourism can clearly be an important potential or existing contributor to the local economy, it should not be seen as the main source of income for households. Full dependency on tourism would be extremely risky. A responsible approach to tourism positions tourism as an additional and complementary livelihood strategy at the household level.

Guidance on Completing Tourism Value Chain and Pro-poor Impact Analysis

This annex provides practical guidance on the systematic process of analysing the current impact of tourism on poverty in the destination, with implications for prioritising future action. It expands on table 1 in section 1.4 and explains how to complete each stage.

1 Conduct initial stakeholder interviews and consultation	At the outset, talk to some of the main players, including those within the DM group as well as those outside it, to form a broad picture of tourism in the destination and the issues for its development. Concentrate on: • The Tourism Board (or equivalent) locally and nationally. • The local authority(ies) – if appropriate, at different levels. • The main tour operators handling visitors in the destination, who often have the best feel for how it functions and the issues involved. • Representative bodies of the different types of tourism service providers. In addition to the above, consider holding an initial workshop which brings together a wider range of stakeholders. This workshop, which might last a full day, should involve facilitated group working sessions in which people: • reveal their level of knowledge of tourism in the destination, or lack of it, and share ideas on sources of information; • work together to develop a conceptual map of the destination's tourism value chain – of the range of tourism resources and supply chain linkages; • share information on markets and trends – who are the current tourists to the destination and how is this changing?; • consider the main beneficiaries (current and desired – see 1.3) of tourism in the destination; • list barriers to progress and brainstorm on the main issues to address.
2 Create an inventory of tourism facilities and services	Make a list of known providers of tourism facilities and services in the destination. This should include tour operators, accommodation, restaurants used by tourists, visitor attractions, activity providers, transport providers, handicraft sellers, guides, and other relevant services. Many destinations have surprisingly incomplete data on the actual supply of tourism services in the area. You will need to pull together information from a range of sources, including existing lists, published guidebooks, personal knowledge and observation. Also, be sure to ask tour operators about their knowledge of local facilities. In making the inventory: • cover services/facilities relating to the whole visitor journey from pre arrival to after departure; • concentrate on services used by tourists, not just locals – but bear in mind the domestic as well as international markets; • include basic information on the facility or service. In particular include: size (e.g. number of rooms); location; grade; price; ownership; contact details; • group some types of service together if it is impractical to list suppliers individually, but give an indication of the total numbers involved; • make sensible estimates if you can't be precise – e.g. on number of taxi operators.

3 Assemble market and performance knowledge	Collect together any available information about the performance of tourism in the destination, including: annual growth/decline and seasonal patterns, the source markets, types of visitor, occupancy of accommodation, amount and type of recent or planned investment. This may be available from: • published statistics – however, look closely at the source, date and reliability; • information provided during the initial consultation; • visitor arrival data – possibly from transport providers; • previous visitor surveys; • admission data from the main paid attractions. You may find that relevant information on markets and trends is available at a national or regional level rather than locally. This can still be used to build up a picture of the likely situation and opportunities in the destination. This initial assemblage of information can be added to subsequently from the following steps of the process, outlined below.
4 Identify types of job/ activity most relevant to the target poor	At this stage and before going further with the analysis it will be necessary to consider how you will distinguish between tourism activities that are delivering benefit to the poor and those that are not doing so. This step is essentially about helping you decide what to look out for in the research and analysis. First, consider who constitutes the poor in the destination and those you may wish to target. This has been covered in the section 1.3 of this manual. These poor may be local people (living in the destination) who may be, for example: • living in particular types of location; • generally unskilled or semi-skilled; • women, or from particular indigenous or ethnic groups; • people with other forms of disadvantage. In the analysis, it will not be possible to directly count the number of poor, or previously poor, people involved in tourism. You will not be able to ask them directly about their poverty. Therefore you should concentrate on what is identifiable, using some proxy measures as appropriate. Make a list of what to identify and measure in your research and analysis. This should include: • Jobs that are undertaken by and/or accessible to the above types of poor people. • Income flows that reach and benefit them, e.g. through the supply chain.
5 Identify sub-chains and categorise enterprises/service	Steps 1-4 will have enabled you to obtain an initial impression of the structure of the tourism value chain in the area. You may at this stage wish to distinguish: • Particular parts or aspects of the tourism value chain that you believe most likely to be of relevance to the future development of tourism in general, and to poverty alleviation in particular. hese are sometimes referred to as sub-chains. An example might be a particular part of the tourism offer (e.g. diving or mountain climbing). • Types of tourism enterprise or service that could be targeted in subsequent work, depending on the extent to which you believe they may already be, or could become, pro-poor (e.g. luxury hotels or handicraft makers). This preliminary selection will largely be based on instinct or intuition, but may offer a way to focus the organization of subsequent investigations and eventual action.

6 Conduct enterprise survey/interviews	Based on steps 1, 2 and 5, a sample of tourism enterprises should be selected for survey. These should be representative of the various categories of enterprise, with a good spread of size, ownership type etc. They should include accommodation, food and beverage enterprises, activity/excursion providers and retailers, although this may vary depending on the sub-chain(s) selected for investigation. Avoid selecting just those that you feel most likely to be pro-poor. At least some enterprises should be interviewed face to face, but others may be provided with survey forms to complete. Tour operators may be able to provide some of this information from their own knowledge of the enterprises that they use - this may help you save time. In order to maximise results and efficiency, you should inform the enterprises of the exercise in advance and gain their interest and support. Surveys/interviews should cover: • Details of the enterprise – size, services, grade, price, ownership etc. • Performance – occupancy, seasonality, indication of turnover and profitability; past and future planned investment. • Human resources – number and type of jobs (indicating if full time or part time), pay levels and treatment of tips/gratuities, source of labour (eg whether from poor communities), gender of staff, skills required, training provided, turnover of staff, recruitment policy and issues, potential for future job growth. • Sourcing and procurement of produce, services etc. – approximate amount spent on different items; whether sources are local and/or from poor communities. • Community engagement – sponsorship and other voluntary assistance given to poor communities; development or maintenance of infrastructure that may help poor communities; relationship with local informal economy. • Any barriers/problems that they face with respect to benefiting the poor (e.g. inhibitors to purchasing from the poor such as quality and reliability). • Issues affecting future tourism development in the enterprise and destination. Priority should be given to surveying direct service providers of the kind listed above. However, if time and resources permit, you should also survey a sample of the main secondary suppliers, such as food wholesalers and producers, to find out the extent to which their activities benefit the poor.
7 Conduct a visitor survey	A survey of visitors can provide very helpful information to guide destination management and also to understand more about the level, nature and flow of tourism spending by different types of tourist. It can provide a cross-bearing on the enterprise survey results. In practice: • Surveys should be based on short face to face interviews. • The number of completed questionnaires to aim for may vary from around 100 to over 500 depending on the size of destination, the total number of visitors and practical constraints. Lower numbers can provide a broad feel for visitor response and higher numbers more accuracy for quantified results. • It is best to reach visitors at the end of their stay, in order to record actual activities, so surveying should preferably take place at exit points. However, it could also happen at main visitor sites, with some initial filter questions to avoid people who have just arrived. Questions should: • Cover general issues to inform destination management: visitor profile (age, origin, whether in a group; etc.); itinerary in the country; activities in the destination (use of transport, accommodation, guiding, visits to attractions, use of information, etc.); attitudes to the destination (satisfaction/dissatisfaction, any recommendations for improvement).

7 Conduct a visitor survey	• Probe visitor spending patterns and levels: length of stay; total spent per person per day; package and discretionary spending (accommodation, food, crafts/souvenirs, transport, guides/excursions, etc. including tips/gratuities); issues affecting spending. • Obtain feedback on experiences and attitudes particularly relevant to poverty alleviation – e.g. concern about impact of spending, interest in supporting poor communities and in relevant products, preparedness to donate, etc.
8 Aggregate results	Data can be selected from the information gathered through the above steps which can be brought together to enable you to estimate, very approximately, the total amount of visitor spending in the destination, where it is going (eg by sector or by sub-chain), and the proportion of each different type of expenditure that is benefiting the poor. Each destination will need to look across the raw data that has been collected and consider how they can best use it in their circumstances and for their particular purposes. However, some broadly relevant procedures are as follows: • Group questionnaires/data from the enterprise survey (step 6) according to different types of enterprise in which you are interested, thinking particularly about the sub-chains and categories (step 5). This could be by sector (eg accommodation or craft-sellers) or by selecting enterprises associated with a particular product (eg a trek or tour). For each type of enterprise, look at the evidence on employment, suppliers etc. This should enable you to make a rough estimate of the percentage of visitor spending on that type of enterprise that finds its way to the poor (i.e. is pro-poor). • From the inventory (step 2), estimate the total number of enterprises of each type in the destination. Multiply this by an estimate of average annual turnover for each type of enterprise, calculated from the enterprise survey (step 6), to get an estimate of the annual contribution of that group of enterprises to the value of tourism in the destination. • Using the results from your previous calculation, multiply this value by the percentage that is pro-poor, to get an estimate of the annual contribution of that type of tourism enterprise, sector or product, to the poor. • Combine results across all types of enterprise to arrive at the total pro-poor income estimate for the destination. • Using the visitor survey (step 7) look at the proportion of spending by different kinds of visitor on different types of enterprise or activity. (Where product is commonly sold as a package, it may be possible to obtain this information from tour operators (step 6). The visitor survey can then serve as a means of validating data obtained elsewhere and will also provide information on discretionary spending. • Combine this with the results above to form a view of the types of visitor and types of activity that are more or less pro-poor in their impact. • Look at the evidence from the enterprise survey (step 6) and stakeholder discussions (step 1) to consider in which ways the poor are mainly benefiting. This might be through employment, direct spending, secondary sourcing, etc. • Use all of the results that you have produced through interrogating your data to consider the types of products or clusters that may be more or less pro-poor. Revisit the groupings and sub-chains that you identified in step 5 as potentially pro-poor in their impact. In tourism, it is not always clear where in the value chain to expect the poor to participate – there is no prior assumption that a certain kind of tourism or part of the supply chain will offer most benefit to the poor.
9 Draw conclusions	The aggregated results, together with the qualitative feedback and knowledge obtained from the stakeholder consultation and the enterprise and visitor surveys, will enable conclusions to be drawn about future opportunities and priority areas for intervention that have the potential to significantly expand income and opportunities for the poor. section 1.6 of this manual shows how the detailed results from this analysis can be applied in focussing interventions and actions.

Further Considerations on Product Identification and Sales

Adapted from inputs to UNWTO *Seminar on Tourism and Poverty Alleviation,*
Arusha, Tanzania, Harol Goodwin, 2006

A. Identifying potential products for sale to existing tourists

An audit needs to be conducted of the potential tourism assets. The process should engage local tourism and other business people, cultural workers, guides, domestic and international operators or their representatives, some dialogue with tourists in the destination and the potential poor producers themselves. It is particularly important that the views of private sector operators and of tourists are taken into account in evaluating potential goods and services. This analysis will generally need to be sophisticated enough to consider different market sectors, according to what types of tourists are visiting the area.

Goods and services produced by the local community and poor producers are unlikely to constitute the core product of an area, motivating international or domestic tourists to travel to the destination. They are more likely to be supporting resources or complementary products, contributing to the overall appeal of the destination.

The purpose of the audit is to identify those goods and services which could be developed by the local community and which will be attractive to the kinds of tourists already coming to the area. It is therefore important to bear in mind the available market (the tourists and day excursionists in the local area) and the resources available to, and required by, the local community and/or poor producers in order to develop and supply the potential goods and services. The following list of suggestions is not exhaustive but it is helpful in identifying the kinds of services and products which could be considered.

Suggested framework to assist in identifying potential products

Natural Resources	Cultural
• Guided walks to natural features	• Old buildings and sites
• Natural foods and traditional medicines	• Traditional ways of life – cooking, farming, forestry
• Traditional craft	• Music, dance, story telling
• Farming	• Dress, folklore and traditions
• Fishing	• Arts and craft
• Horticulture	• Food and drink
• Bee keeping	• Religious buildings, sites and practises
• Mariculture	• School visits
Activities and Events	**Tourism Services**
• Local festivals and fairs	• Guiding
• Music festivals	• Backpacker accommodation
• Fishing, boating, kayaking	• Homestays
• Traditional and contemporary sports	• Local produce
• Traditional and local markets	• Drinks and meals

In constructing the audit and making the resource inventory, it is important to consider the following questions in order to identify opportunities.

1. How unique or special is the proposed product or service to the area, does it relate to the place?

2. How significant is the market when judged by the different types of tourists who already frequent the area?

3. Are there issues of quality or continuity of supply?

4. Are there social or cultural sensitivities about sharing or selling the product or service to the tourists?

5. Are there issues of seasonality affecting the product or service, or the tourist flow?

6. Are there any access issues?

7. How does the proposed product or service fit with existing products and services?

8. Are there actual or perceived safety issues?

9. How might the proposed product or service be improved?

B. Factors that encourage the purchasing of arts, local crafts and food[1]

Experience in a number of different destinations suggests that there are a range of things which can be done to encourage tourists to spend money purchasing goods. The suggestions here draws on experience in several countries in Africa, Asia and Caribbean.

Local craft sales are boosted by:

- products specific to the destination;

- more production on-site, at the stalls;

- a range of differentiated products: not all vendors selling the same;

- product innovation: combining local skills with modern preferences (e.g. in the Gambia, women make Gambian dresses for Barbie dolls!);

- less hassle of tourists: harassment stops sales;

- price information for tourists (a range within which haggling is acceptable);

- better quality products;

- better presentation of products;

- ensuring products can be packed and are transportable;

- sales of locally-made products inside hotels;

- labelling and interpretation to tell 'the story' and thus add value;

- tailor-made items made to order (e.g. personalised with names, garments made to size);

- code of conduct among sellers governing behaviour, prices, location, management of environmental impacts of materials used;

---

1   From Ashley et al., 2006.

- art and craft areas or clusters, where tourists can see producers and competition drives innovation;

- reputation and popularity (the idea of must-have souvenirs).

Local food and drink sales are boosted by:

- ensuring product quality and standards;

- exploiting smells, flavours, tastes and niche preferences (e.g. organic coffee and chocolate);

- opportunities to mix with locals;

- area of origin ("terroire") labels: brands that guarantee tourists authenticity, local sourcing and recognised quality;

- local festivals.

Local market visits are boosted by:

- local colour;

- range of products;

- opportunities to see producers at work;

- reliable transport;

- opportunities to mix with locals.

Local guiding is boosted by:

- availability of specialist guides (e.g. in birding, agricultural tours);

- licensing or system of official recognition;

- agreed pricing that is made available to tourists in writing.

Indicators Relating to the Seven Mechanisms

Prepared by UNWTO, 2008

1. Employment		
A. Indicators on benefits from tourism	**B. Indicators on enabling environment and support activities**	**C. Indicators on perception/ satisfaction by stakeholders**
• Number and % of workers in the community directly employed in tourism (% full time, % part time). • Ratio (or%) of locals to "outsiders" directly employed in tourism. • % local tourism workers employed at different skill levels (unskilled, technical, administrative, middle/senior management, contract). • Ratio of men to women employed directly in tourism occupations. • % indigenous people employed directly in tourism (if appropriate). • Earnings in tourism employment (hourly, daily, monthly, annually), compared with earning in other sources of livelihood (e.g. agriculture, fishing, manufacturing). Distribution of income throughout the year. • Number of enterprises providing non-monetary benefits to poor employees (e.g. in-kind giving's, access to recreational facilities, transportation). • Number of enterprises offering social benefits and services: e.g. health insurance or services, access to education, provision of sanitary services, and other infrastructure. Number, % of staff benefiting. This point I also relevant to mechanism n. 7 on social services stimulated by tourism.	• Existence of institutions and programmes offering vocational training for tourism employment (organized by colleges and schools, government, development agencies) in the destination area. Level of participation of community members in these programmes. • Number of enterprises with clearly defined policies on local sourcing of employees. • Existence of staff in charge of community-relations in the enterprises. • Number of enterprises offering on-the-job training, % of staff participating. • Existence of saving schemes and programmes to distribute the use of income from tourism throughout the year.	• % of community members satisfied with employment opportunities, conditions. • % of employees with the opinion that the earnings and benefits from tourism can sufficiently support family and livelihood needs. • % of employees relying completely or partially on tourism employment for livelihood needs. • % of employees satisfied with the training opportunities and programmes. • % of tourists satisfied with the quality, attitude and attendance by employees.

2. Supply chain		
A. Indicators on benefits from tourism	**B. Indicators on enabling environment and support activities**	**C. Indicators on perception/ satisfaction by stakeholders**
• % of supply of tourism enterprises sourced from local producers and service providers (subdivided by types of goods and services, such as food, building material and décor, transportation and guiding services, etc.) • % of locally produced goods and services sold to tourism enterprises.	• % of enterprises with clear policies on local sourcing, or with programmes and partnerships supporting local producers. • Existence of capacity building and technical assistance programmes for local supply development. Level of participation. • Existence of financial incentives (e.g. grant, soft loans, etc.) and extension services to facilitate local suppliers. Level of participation.	• % of local suppliers satisfied with the collaboration with tourism businesses. • % of local suppliers satisfied with the capacity building activities, and financial incentives. • •% of local suppliers with the opinion that sales in tourism sufficiently support family and livelihood needs. • % of enterprises satisfied with the quality of local produce, products and services. • % of tourists satisfied with locally supplied products and services.
3. Informal selling		
A. Indicators on benefits from tourism	**B. Indicators on enabling environment and support activities**	**C. Indicators on perception/ satisfaction by stakeholders**
• Number of vendors (estimate) and variety of goods and services sold to tourists. • Earnings through direct sales (hourly, daily, monthly, annual), compared with earning in other sources of livelihood (e.g. agriculture, fishing, manufacturing).	• Existence of special areas at destinations for informal vendors. • Existence of association and/or register of vendors and service providers (e.g. handicraft sellers, guides), and number of members. • Existence of capacity building, financial, and technical assistance programmes directed to vendors and their associations. Level of participation. • Existence of regulation, coordination and conflict resolution mechanisms between vendors, tourism enterprises, local authorities and other stakeholders involved.	• % of local suppliers with the opinion that sales in tourism sufficiently support family and livelihood needs. • Number of tourists, tourism enterprises complaining on harassment y informal vendors. • Number, % of tourists purchasing from informal vendors, level of spendings.

4. Enterprise development		
A. Indicators on benefits from tourism	**B. Indicators on enabling environment and support activities**	**C. Indicators on perception/ satisfaction by stakeholders**
• Number of tourism-related MSMEs operating in the community (subdivided by types, e.g. accommodation and catering, guiding, transportation, tour operation, etc.). • Number of community members employed by MSMEs, number of families supported by MSMEs. • Incentives for MSMEs (e.g. special credits, tax advantage, grants, legal conditions, etc.): availability, level provided/used. • Return on investment in MSMEs (month or year). • Longetivity/duration/turnover of businesses. • Capacity building for establishment and improvement of MSMEs: number of programmes/events, level of participation. • Earnings of SME employees (hourly, daily, monthly, annually), compared with earning in other sources of livelihood (e.g. agriculture, fishing, manufacturing).* • Net profits of tourism SMEs, as compared to local small businesses in other sectors.*	• Existence of SME business associations, number/& of businesses participating. • Existence of capacity building programmes (training, advisory services), number of businesses benefiting. • Existence of economic incentives for business development (e.g. soft loans, microcredit's, grants), amount of funds involved and disbursed, number of businesses benefiting • Existence of marketing and other support activities (e.g. web-based mechanisms, inclusion in general marketing activities and material, collective marketing). • Partnerships beween SMEs, communty enterprises and businesses (e.g. TOs). • Existence of income and benefit distribution mechanisms in community.based tourism projects (e.g. rotation of staff, community fund, investment in public infrastructure and services).	• % of businesses satisfied with results, with positive or negative perspectives for future development. • % of businesses satisfied with business support programmes and activities (access, ease of participation, usefulness, effectiveness). • % of tourists satisfied with the services of SMEs. • % of tourism companies and operators satisfied with SME partners.
5. Tax/charge		
A. Indicators on benefits from tourism	**B. Indicators on enabling environment and support activities**	**C. Indicators on perception/ satisfaction by stakeholders**
• % and volume of tourism tax and levy retained by the local authority/community. • % and volume of tourism tax and levy spent on local infrastructure development or social programmes.	• Existence of policies and regulations facilitating the application and local retention of tourism levies and taxes. • % and volume of tourism tax and levy spent on capacity building, tourism SME support, the conservation of tourist attractions and other tourism development programmes.	• Level of satisfaction by local authorities, communities on applying and using income generated through taxes and levies.

6. Voluntary giving		
A. Indicators on benefits from tourism	**B. Indicators on enabling environment and support activities**	**C. Indicators on perception/ satisfaction by stakeholders**
• Number of enterprises providing voluntary supports, or encouraging tourists to donate. • Number of community-support projects (per type, like education, health, infrastructure), and number of community members/ families benefiting from them. • Number/% of tourists donating for community development projects, amount provided. • Monetary value of voluntary giving/support per year.	• Number of enterprises with clearly established community outreach policies and programmes, and with staff designated to community relations. • Existence of clearly defined donation schemes, mechanism to generate and manage funds raised through charity by tourists. • Existence of clear communications by companies encouraging tourists to donate for community development and conservation activities.	• Level of satisfaction by local communities on community development programmes supported by tourism companies. • Number of tourists indicate willingness to donate to community development projects. • Level of satisfaction of tourists the way donations are handled and communicated.
7. Collateral benefit		
A. Indicators on benefits from tourism	**B. Indicators on enabling environment and support activities**	**C. Indicators on perception/ satisfaction by stakeholders**
• Value of investment in infrastructure and social services (total and per type of infrastructure and services). • Number of community members and families benefiting from the infrastructure and social service development. • Social improvements attributed to tourism infrastructure development: number (or%) of local population with access to water, electricity, sanitary system, telecommunication, to education and health services. • Tourist access infrastructure and services (via land, water or air) developed benefiting also transportation and communication of locals.	• Existence of investment policies and regulations favouring access of local communities to tourism-related infrastructure. • Number of companies with clear policy on community-support activities in social services.	• Level of satisfaction by local community on infrastructure development projects related to tourism (% thinks it benefits the community, or hinders community access to areas and resources). • Level of satisfaction by tourism companies and developers on policies and regulations related to infrastructure development.

Suggestions for a Training Programme

The material presented in this manual can be used for training purposes. This Appendix provides an indicative programme of training sessions which could be adapted for use in different situations.

The kinds of participants that could be invited to a training workshop(s) might include:

- those working in the field of tourism at the destination level;

- those working more widely at this level to support poverty alleviation, including NGOs and advisory bodies;

- local government officials and those working in other public sector agencies;

- private sector operators who have demonstrated an interest in these issues.

This has been designed as a three day programme, which can be delivered as one block or spread over three separate days. It is not necessary to include every step in every workshop. This is a menu from which workshop organisers can select the tasks which they see as most relevant to the circumstances of the participants. However, steps should be kept in the same broad sequence as they are designed to follow a logical progression.

There may be some circumstances in which all participants will be drawn from one single destination which is the focus of their interest. In others, individuals from several different destinations within one country or region may be gathered together for training purposes.

This may affect the dynamic and format of the workshop sessions. Where all participants are focused on a single destination (referred to as 'single destination workshop' – SDW), the training workshop can itself form a part of the analysis and action-planning process. Exercises will provide an opportunity to work together on tasks that are based on common knowledge of issues that are specific to the destination, and around which a shared understanding can be developed. It may be feasible to plan the workshop in separate time blocks, with an intervening opportunity for participants to develop work on key tasks or 'Take-away tasks'.

If possible, one or two days could be added to the training programme for field work in the destination to give the participants the possibility to apply the concepts and tools presented during the training. The participants can carry out the field work in sub-groups and present their findings in plenary sessions.

Where participants are drawn from several destinations (referred to as 'multiple destination workshop' - MDW), training is more likely to be delivered in one block. Exercises will need to offer a mix of opportunities to work as an individual on specific local issues and opportunities to share findings, ideas and concerns in pairs or small groups.

Material for the input to each session should be drawn from the relevant section in the main body of the manual.

Detailed instructions are presented for each exercise, including any preparation required. The exercises outlined here are only suggestions. Workshop organisers may not wish to include an exercise in every session and can adapt the exercises suggested or add others of their own.

The ideal size for a training workshop is perhaps 15-30 participants, in order to assemble a range of experiences and outlooks but also to allow everyone to be fully engaged. However, all tasks can be adapted for a smaller or larger group.

Suggested programme

Session	Content of session	Section in manual
Day 1		
Introduction		
1	Overview of workshop/introduce participants	Intro
2	Input: Introduction to Tourism and Poverty Alleviation. **Exercise 1** – 10 principles for pursuing poverty alleviation through tourism.	Intro
Part One: Destination Management for Poverty Alleviation		
3	Input: Introduction to destination management as basis for work on poverty alleviation. **Exercise 2** – Thinking about destinations.	1
4	Input: Introduction to a pro-poor approach to destination management. **Exercise 3** – Seven step approach.	1
5	Input: Importance of national policy in supporting poverty alleviation through tourism. **Exercise 4** – Ensuring supportive national policies.	1.1
6	Input: Stakeholders in destination management. **Exercise 5** – Who is already involved?	1.2
7	Input: Who are the target beneficiaries and what are their needs group. **Group discussion**	1.3
Optional take-away task: Investigate the sources of statistics on poverty in your destination. Bring back a short paper outlining the target beneficiaries that you have identified.		
Day 2		
1	Input: Introduction to the tourism value chain for a destination. **Exercise 6** - Unpicking a tourism value chain.	1.4
2	Input: Steps in analysing a tourism value chain and its pro-poor impact. **Exercise 7**– Using an enterprise survey to investigate pro-poor impact.	1.4
3	Input: Presentation on the process of aggregating results. **Exercise 8** – Examining the results from the process.	1.4
4	Input: The destination's potential for tourism that benefits the poor (1). **Exercise 9** – An approach to markets and products.	1.5
5	Input: The destination's potential for tourism that benefits the poor (2). **Exercise 10** – SWOT analysis of a destination's potential to benefit the poor.	1.5
6	Input: Strategic choices from a pro-poor perspective. **Exercise 11** – Making some strategic choices. Input: Introduction to the three main objectives as a basis for choosing interventions.	1.6
7	Input: Strengthening stakeholder capacity and response. **Exercise 12** – Working with stakeholders to develop their capacity.	1.7
Optional take-away task: Prepare a handout setting out the three objectives and the pro-poor growth model (figure 4, section 1.6). Instruction: Think about how the objectives and the model relate to your own destination. Bring back one example of each product type (A, B, C) which you think might offer pro-poor growth potential in your destination.		

Session	Content of session	Section in manual
Day 3		
Part Two: Mechanisms for Reaching the Poor		
1	Input: Introduction to the 7 mechanisms. **Exercise 13** – Who needs to make the effort? **Exercise 14** – Which mechanisms to consider?	2
	At this point, it is suggested that the previous session is used to select one or two mechanisms which are of particular interest to the group. The next two sessions should be devoted to these mechanisms. Alternatively, several small groups could each choose a different mechanism to work on in parallel.	
2	Input: A chance to focus on one particular mechanism. **Exercise 15** – Focus on first selected mechanism.	2.X
3	Input: A chance to focus on another particular mechanism. **Exercise 16** – Focus on second selected mechanism.	2.Y
Part Three: Indicators and Measurement of Impact		
4	Input: Selecting indicators and monitoring processes.	
	Exercise 17 – Selecting indicators.	3

Workshop material (the workshop material is enclosed to this book)

Exercise 1 10 Principles for pursuing poverty alleviation through tourism (see p. xvii)

Prepare:

- 10 cards with one principle on each, unseen (work sheet 1).

Instruction:

- Each person takes a card and looks at it.

In turn, each person reads out their principle and **briefly** says what they think it means and gives an example from their experience of 1) where they have seen this to be true and 2) where they believe that this has not happened.

Exercise 2 Thinking about destinations

Think about the parts of your own area which could be described as a tourist destination. Discuss in pairs (MDW) or small groups (SDW):

- Does it meet the criteria identified in terms of identity, size and the range of services available?

- How would you define the destination – what are its boundaries?

- Should it be linked to other areas for some purposes?

- Are there distinctive smaller areas or communities within the destination that you may wish to work with?

Exercise 3 Seven step approach

Prepare:

- Copies of a single sheet (MDW) or flipchart (SDW) with the following table (work sheet 2).

Instruction:

- MDW: Complete alone and discuss in pairs.

- SDW: Complete and discuss as a group or in small groups.

Table for exercise 3

Step	How important is this to you? 5 = very important 1 = not at all important	Has this step been taken already? 5 = completely 1 = not at all
1. Ensuring supportive national policies		
2. Working effectively with different stakeholders		
3. Identifying who should benefit and their needs		
4. Understanding how tourism is working currently and who is benefiting		
5. Judging the destination's future potential for tourism that benefits the poor		
6. Agreeing on a strategy and action plan to alleviate poverty through tourism		
7. Strengthening stakeholder response and capacity		

Exercise 4 Ensuring supportive national policies

- SDW: Discuss as one group or small groups.

- MDW: Discuss in pairs.

Think about the attention paid to the relationship between tourism and poverty alleviation at a national level in your country.

- List the Ministries that you think have a role to play in this. Do they get together to discuss tourism and coordinate policy and action?

- Do you know what the Poverty Reduction Strategy says about tourism?

- Is there a National Tourism Strategy and is poverty alleviation recognised as a key objective?

Consider the decentralisation of policies and action to support tourism development and management in your country.

- Is this encouraged and supported by national policy?

- To what extent are local government structures encouraged and resourced to support tourism?

- Have specific destination management areas been identified and would this be helpful?

Exercise 5 Who is already involved?

Prepare:

- Handout of figure 2 (section 1.2) indicating range of stakeholders in destination management (work sheet 3).

- Copies of a single sheet (MDW) or flipchart (SDW) with the following table (work sheet 4).

Instruction:

- MDW: Complete alone and discuss in pairs.

- SDW: Complete and discuss as a group or in small groups.

Table for exercise 5

Stakehoder type	Who does this mean for your destination?	Who is already involved?	Who is not yet involved?
National government			
Regional government			
District authority/municipality			
International tour operators			
National/local tour operators			
Tourist service providers			
Local residents			
NGOs and assistance agencies			
Tourists			
Other?			

Exercise 6 Unpicking a tourism value chain

Prepare:

- Handout of figure 3 (section 1.4) showing the tourism value chain (work sheet 5).

Instruction:

- SDW: Work in small groups.

- MDW: Work in pairs.

Pick one particular component of the visitor experience (for example sleeping or shopping) and write out the chain of (some of the) suppliers involved with delivering that experience in your destination (or one you know well). Have a first go at thinking about which points in the supply chain you think might be most likely to benefit the poor.

Exercise 7 Using an enterprise survey to investigate pro-poor impact

- SDW/MDW: Work in pairs to draw up six questions that you would want to include in an enterprise questionnaire to investigate the pro-poor impact of **accommodation** in a destination.

Bring them back to the group and invite each pair to share one of their questions. Record on a flip chart and keep adding different questions until they have all been included. Talk about what you have assembled. Could this be turned into an enterprise survey for self-completion or would it work better as a face-to-face interview? What resources would you need and who would provide them?

Exercise 8 Examining the results from the aggregation process

Prepare:

- Handout from box 5 (section 1.4) showing a value chain analysis calculation (work sheet 6).

Instruction:

- Discuss as a group what it is showing. Consider the influence of both the **volume** of spending and the **proportion** of spending reaching the poor. In what components of spending would a marginal change in (a) visitor spending and (b) pro-poor policies and actions, have the greatest impact on the poor?

Exercise 9 An approach to markets and products

Prepare:

- Handout of table 2 (section 1.5), based on Ansoff's Matrix (work sheet 7).

- Copies of the following 'blank' matrix (work sheet 8).

- SDW/MDW: Discuss in pairs a destination that you know to complete the 'blank' Product-Market Matrix with illustrations of each product-market mix, thinking about the likely success of each combination in contributing to poverty alleviation.

Table for Exercise 9 Product-Market Matrix

Market		Product	
		EXISTING	**NEW**
EXISTING		1 **Market penetration**	2 **Product development**
NEW		3 **Market development**	4 **Diversification**

Work Sheet 1 – Exercise 1

10 Principles for pursuing poverty alleviation through tourism

1   All aspects and types of tourism can and should be concerned about poverty alleviation.

2   All governments should include poverty alleviation as a key aim of tourism development and consider tourism as a possible tool for alleviating poverty.

3   The competitiveness and economic success of tourism businesses and destinations is critical to poverty alleviation – without this the poor cannot benefit.

4   All tourism businesses should be concerned about the impact of their activities on local communities and seek to benefit the poor through their actions.

5   Tourism destinations should be managed with poverty alleviation as a central aim that is built into strategies and action plans.

6   A sound understanding of how tourism functions in destinations is required, including how tourism income is distributed and who benefits from this.

7   Planning and development of tourism in destinations should involve a wide range of interests, including participation and representation from poor communities.

8   All potential impacts of tourism on the livelihood of local communities should be considered, including current and future local and global impacts on natural and cultural resources.

9   Attention must be paid to the viability of all projects involving the poor, ensuring access to markets and maximising opportunities for beneficial links with established enterprises.

10   Impacts of tourism on poverty alleviation should be effectively monitored.

Work Sheet 2 – Exercise 3

Table for exercise 3

Step	How important is this to you? 5 = very important 1 = not at all important	Has this step been taken already? 5 = completely 1 = not at all
1. Ensuring supportive national policies		
2. Working effectively with different stakeholders		
3. Identifying who should benefit and their needs		
4. Understanding how tourism is working currently and who is benefiting		
5. Judging the destination's future potential for tourism that benefits the poor		
6. Agreeing on a strategy and action plan to alleviate poverty through tourism		
7. Strengthening stakeholder response and capacity		

Work Sheet 3 – Exercise 5

Figure for exercise 5 – The spread of stakeholders

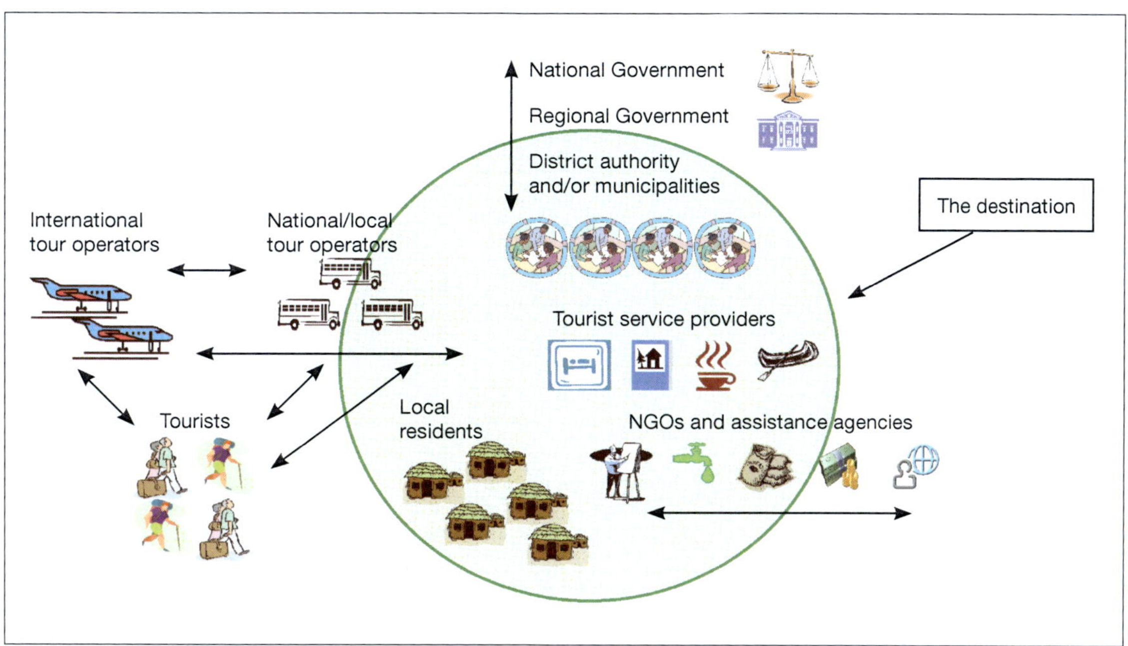

Work Sheet 4 – Exercise 5

Table for exercise 5

Stakehoder type	Who does this mean for your destination?	Who is already involved?	Who is not yet involved?
National government			
Regional government			
District authority/municipality			
International tour operators			
National/local tour operators			
Tourist service providers			
Local residents			
NGOs and assistance agencies			
Tourists			
Other?			

Work Sheet 5 – Exercise 6

Figure for exercise 5 – A tourism value chain for a destination visit

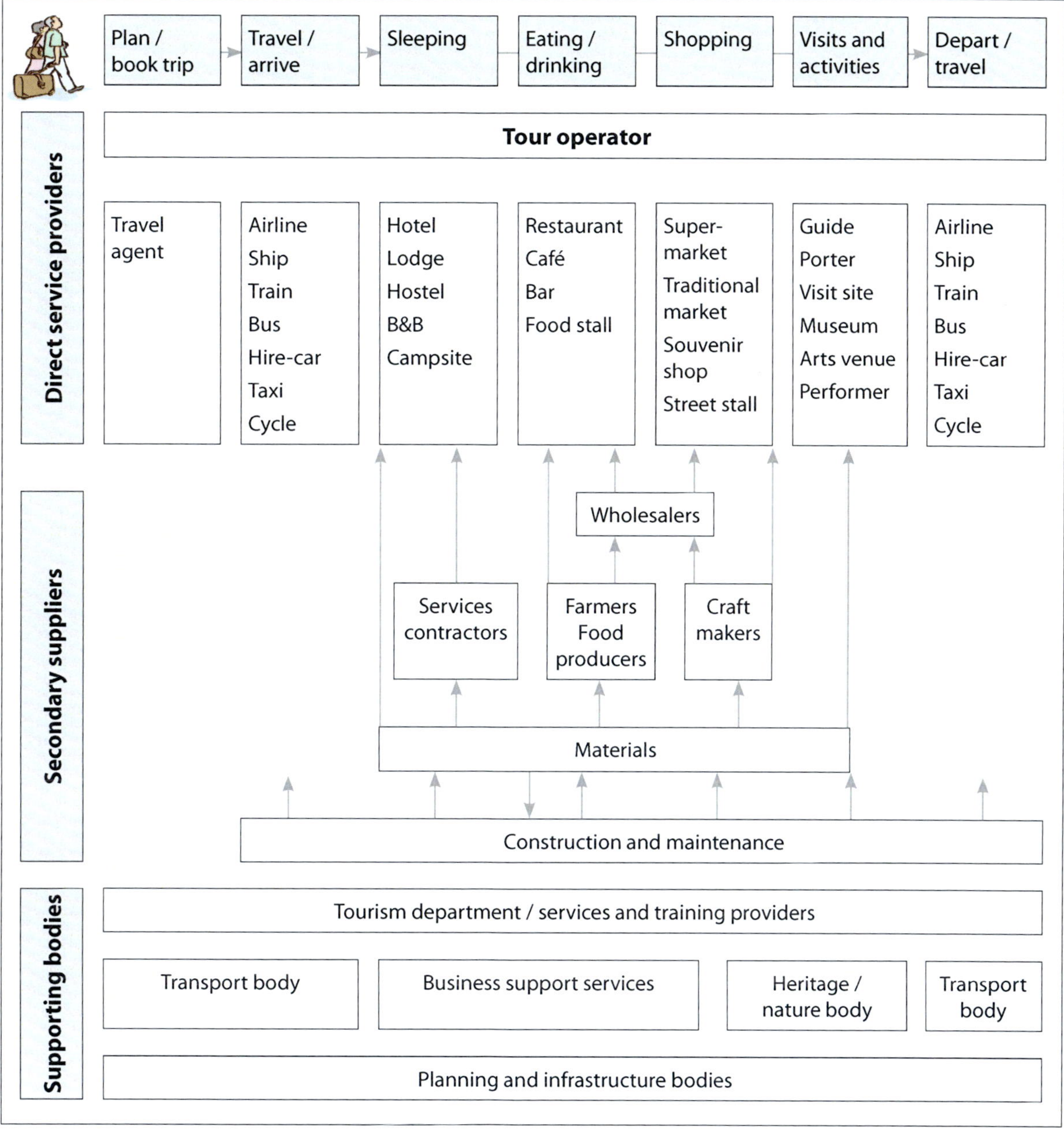

Work Sheet 6 – Exercise 8 (1/2)

Taken from Box 5: Tracing the Tourism Dollar in Northern Tanzania

Tourism in Tanzania is largely concentrated in the north of the country. Working with SNV, the Overseas Development Institute (ODI) analysed the impact on the poor of the tourism value chain associated with various tourism activities. One of these was mountain climbing on Kilimanjaro, a particularly important tourist product.

They used a rapid appraisal technique, developed by ODI, involving:

- Structured interviews with tourism service providers, including tour operators, based at key geographic locations.

- A survey of tourists departing from Kilimanjaro International Airport, having completed their holiday.

The information gathered was synthesised to produce a pro-poor analysis of the value chain for the product, and an estimate was made of the pro-poor impact of each component of tourist expenditure. The table below has been constructed from the results for the Kilimanjaro trek.

Based on the annual number of people participating in climbing Kilimanjaro, it is possible to get an idea of the overall impact of the product on poverty alleviation.

More detailed consideration of visitor spend on each component of the tourism experience and the extent to which that particular expenditure is considered pro-poor make it possible to understand the relative contribution of each component of the tourism experience to poverty alleviation.

The analysis can also be used to identify particular components where marginal changes in activity are most likely to deliver benefits to the poor.

Work Sheet 6 – Exercise 8 (2/2)

Table for exercise 8 – Value chain analysis for Kilimanjaro trek

In-country spend per tourist = cost of package (US$ 1,205) + discretionary spend (US$ 171) = US$ 1,376

Component	Tour operator	Transport	Accommodation	Food and beverage	Cultural goods and services	Wages and tips	Park fees	Total visit
Spend per component	US$ 223	US$ 40	US$ 84	US$ 80	US$ 58	US$ 242	US$ 649	US$ 1,376
Component as % of spend per visit	16%	3%	6%	6%	4%	18%	47%	100%
% of component spend considered pro-poor	0%	0%	16%	90%	50%	100%	5%	-
Pro-poor expenditure per component	-	-	US$ 13	US$ 72	US$ 29	US$ 242	US$ 32	US$ 389
% of total pro-poor expenditure	0%	0%	3%	19%	7%	62%	8%	100%
% of spend per visit which is considered pro-poor								28%

Total annual pro-poor impact of Kilimanjaro trek product:

Number of visits made or packages sold annually	35,000
Total annual in-country expenditure	US$ 50 million
Total annual pro-poor expenditure	US$ 13 million
% of total annual in-country expenditure which is considered pro-poor	28%

Work Sheet 7 – Exercise 9

Table for exercise 9 – Product-market Matrix

		Product	
		EXISTING	**NEW**
Market	**EXISTING**	**1 Market penetration** = Selling more of an existing product to an existing market. Low risk strategy but will supply outstrip demand and lead to price drop and lack of viability?	**2 Product development** = Selling a new or improved product to an existing market. Can stimulate more spending by existing visitors and increase total income to poor communities, but products need to match market interests.
	NEW	**3 Market development** = Selling an existing product to a new market. Can be hard for poor communities to do on their own, but a destination should consider whether there are new markets that it can realistically attract and from which the poor can then benefit.	**4 Diversification** = Selling a new product to a new market. Hard and high risk for poor communities. Would require participation of an established enterprise with a large marketing budget backed by the destination.

Work Sheet 8 – Exercise 9

Table for exercise 9 – Product-market Matrix

<table>
<tr><td colspan="2" rowspan="2"></td><td colspan="2" align="center">Product</td></tr>
<tr><td align="center">EXISTING</td><td align="center">NEW</td></tr>
<tr><td rowspan="2">Market</td><td>EXISTING</td><td>1 Market penetration</td><td>2 Product development</td></tr>
<tr><td>NEW</td><td>3 Market development</td><td>4 Diversification</td></tr>
</table>

Work Sheet 9 – Exercise 10

Table for exercise 10 – SWOT template – showing examples of types of factors to include

Goal: To achieve poverty alleviation through tourism		
	Positive Helpful to achieving the goal	**Negative** Harmful to achieving the goal
Internal Current. Mainly open to control and influence	**Strengths** • Key assets • Available resources • Comparative advantages over competition	**Weaknesses** • Gaps in, or quality of, assets • Resource constraints • Process or funding challenges • Comparative disadvantages
External For future. Mainly beyond direct control	**Opportunities** • Key markets and market trends • Technological advances • Other destinations seeking partners	**Threats** • Political and economic instability • Climate change (sometimes an opportunity) • Strengthening competitors

Work Sheet 10 – Exercise 10

Table for exercise 10 – Goal: To achieve poverty alleviation through tourism

	Positive Helpful to achieving the goal	**Negative** Harmful to achieving the goal
For now mainly **Internal**	**Strengths**	**Weaknesses**
For future mainly **External**	**Opportunities**	**Threats**

Work Sheet 11 – Exercise 11

Table for exercise 11 – Strategic choices and questions from a pro-poor perspective

Strategic choices	Questions to address
The position and relative priority given to tourism in the sustainable development of the destination	• How is tourism performing compared with other economic sectors and livelihood enhancement scenarios? • What alternative options exist for economic growth and poverty alleviation? • Is a focus on tourism justified – should it be stepped up? • Is there a danger of over-dependence on tourism? • Can the integration of tourism with other sectors be improved? • Is tourism, or aspects of it, actually exacerbating poverty – e.g. through depleting resources? • Should the volume of tourism, or some elements of it, be reduced?
The attention given to environmental and socio-cultural impacts	• How serious are environmental and resource use issues in the destination? • How serious are social-cultural issues in the destination? • Can these be addressed by better management of tourism? • Do they restrict the kind of tourism that should be developed?
The degree of focus on particular beneficiaries	• Who should be the main beneficiaries of tourism? • What priority should be given to the poor? • Should priority be given to achieving a volumetric change in poverty levels across the whole destination or to bringing benefit to particular communities? • Should there be a focus on women, certain minorities and disadvantaged groups?
The geographical distribution of tourism in the destination	• Should priority areas and sites for tourism development be identified within the destination? If so, which? • Should attempts be made to bring tourism income/benefit, directly or indirectly, to remote communities?
The selection of target markets	• Which markets are currently delivering the most tourism income in the destination? • Which show greatest potential for growth? • Are these markets also effective in generating spending that reaches the poor (see criteria in section 1.5) or would others be better?
The selection of priority products	• Which current tourism products appear to be delivering most benefit to the poor? • Are these products attractive to the target markets – can they be developed and promoted further? • Can these products be made to be more pro-poor? • Are there other existing products and activities that could be made to be more pro-poor? • What kind of new products and activities can be developed that are good at delivering benefit to the poor?
The setting of targets	• What is a realistic target for the volume of visitors and spending in the destination in five years time? • What is a realistic target for the number of poor households receiving a significant increase in annual income in five years time, and/or having their wellbeing enhanced in other ways, due to tourism (see part 3)?

Work Sheet 12 – Exercise 13

Table for exercise 13 – The role of different players in implementing the mechanisms

Mechanism	Service Enterprises (e.g. hotels)	Tourists and/or Tour Operators	The poor	Local government or DM group
1 Employment of the poor in tourism enterprises.	▲ Active policy of recruitment and training of poor.	Generally support relevant enterprises. Pay fair gratuities.	Look for jobs and participate in training etc.	Provide education and facilitate training and access to jobs.
2 Supply of goods and services to tourism enterprises by the poor.	▲ Active policy of auditing supply chain and sourcing from the poor.	Generally support relevant enterprises and favour local produce etc.	▲ Meet the requirements of enterprises in quality and reliability of supply.	Support suppliers and facilitate linkages and distribution channels.
3 Informal selling of goods and services to tourists by the poor.	Some facilitation – e.g. providing sales points and recommending to guests.	Be prepared to buy from poor – reduce unfair bartering etc.	▲ Provide items to meet demand at right price and quality.	▲ Organise selling, set standards and support improvements.
4 Developing small/micro or community-based tourism enterprises or joint ventures.	▲ Big variation – from no involvement, to mentoring to establishing joint venture partnerships.	Seek out and support relevant enterprises to visit or include in programmes.	▲ Major effort to establish and run enterprises effectively, with potentially high risk.	Provide the right conditions for enterprise formation and help broker partnerships.
5 Tax or charge on tourists or enterprises with proceeds benefiting the poor.	Be prepared to collect/pay the charge and meet the financial burden that this may entail.	Inform tourists of the existence and purpose of any charge .	Engage in the process to maximise receipts for the poor and ensure equitable use of the revenue.	▲ Set up and oversee tax/charge system and use revenue raised to benefit the poor.
6 Voluntary giving by tourists or tourism enterprises that benefits the poor.	Can vary between basic financial support to major engagement with communities.	▲ Requires willingness by tourists and often promotion/ organization by operators.	Receive benefit but and engage in process to ensure equitable use.	Help establish schemes and facilitate links with between recipient communities.
7 Collateral benefits to the poor from tourism investment and activity.	May depend on significant investment and adjustment of plans to meet community needs.	Operators may give some advice/ support at planning stage.	Participation in planning etc. may help to ensure tourism recognises and meets local needs.	▲ Key role in shaping and controlling tourism development to benefit the poor.

Work Sheet 13 – Exercise 14

Handout of mechanisms for exercise 14

1   Employment of the poor in tourism enterprises.

2   Supply of goods and services to tourism enterprises by the poor.

3   Informal selling of goods and services to tourists by the poor.

4   Developing small/micro or community-based tourism enterprises or joint ventures.

5   Tax or charge on tourists or enterprises with proceeds benefiting the poor.

6   Voluntary giving by tourists or tourism enterprises that benefits the poor.

7   Collateral benefits to the poor from tourism investment and activity.

Work Sheet 14 – Exercise 14

Table for exercise 14 – Scenarios for the use of different mechanisms

Situation	Particular mechanisms to consider
Sizeable presence of private sector tourism enterprises – hotels, catering etc. and a nearby large urban/rural poor.	Increasing the proportion of jobs filled by local poor (1) maybe the most sustainable mechanism but there may be limited new jobs available. High volumes of poor may be reachable through supply chains (2) and informal out of pocket spending by tourists (3). Voluntary giving could also help (6).
Relatively remote rural communities with few attractions and little current tourist visitation.	Location may restrict opportunities for direct engagement with tourists and feasible travel to work. Main potential may rest with supply chain (2), but poor could also benefit from general support from taxation revenue (5). In some situations private sector operators may invest in joint ventures (4).
Resort area with high visitation but few established tourism enterprises.	The main opportunity may rest with improving the management of the large amount of informal trading that is likely in such an area, increasing returns from this to the poor (3). Possibly some opportunities to establish some more formal businesses involving the poor (4). Voluntary giving could also help (6).
Poor communities in or near to attractive national park with some visitor throughput and a few established ecolodges.	Various mechanisms may present opportunities here, including establishing community-based initiatives or joint ventures (4), strengthening links with the existing ecolodges (1, 2, 6), and gaining benefit from national park entrance fees (5) or park related infrastructure (7).
Communities with little potential/capacity to engage directly or indirectly in tourism but with clear social deprivation and needs.	Many of the mechanisms could be ruled out here but tourism can still provide benefit to such communities, including schemes that reach the most needy poor, through taxation/charges (5) and more directly via voluntary giving (6) and possibly via collateral benefit such as infrastructure (7).
Area with expanding tourism sector including physical development projects, with a poor local population.	Opportunities may exist here to create the right conditions for new employment (1) and supply chain links (2) to the incoming enterprises, foster associated micro enterprises (4) and ensure collateral benefits to local residents (7).

Exercise 10 SWOT Analysis

Prepare:

- Handout of table 3 (section 1.5) outlining the components of a SWOT analysis (work sheet 9).

- Copies of a single sheet (MDW) or flipchart (SDW) with the following table (work sheet 10).

Instruction:

- MDW: Work alone and discuss in pairs.

- SDW: Work as a group or in small groups.

Complete the template with the factors that apply to your destination.

Table for Exercise 10 Goal: To achieve poverty alleviation through tourism

	Positive Helpful to achieving the goal	**Negative** Harmful to achieving the goal
For now mainly **Internal**	**Strengths**	**Weaknesses**
For future mainly **External**	**Opportunities**	**Threats**

Exercise 11 Making some strategic choices

Prepare:

- Handout of table 4 (section 1.6) outlining the strategic choices to be made, together with associated questions from a pro-poor perspective (work sheet 11).

Instruction:

- MDW: Work in pairs.

- SDW: Work in small groups.

Allocate **one** of the following strategic choices to each pair or group:

1. The position and relative priority given to tourism in the sustainable development of the destination.

2. The degree of focus on particular beneficiaries.

3. The geographical distribution of tourism in the destination.

4. The selection of target markets.

5. The selection of priority products.

For the strategic choice that you have been allocated, and thinking about your own destination, discuss how you would answer the questions to be addressed from a pro-poor perspective. What is the choice(s) that you would recommend for your destination?

Exercise 12 Working with stakeholders to develop their capacity

Instruction:

- Work in pairs. Choose an example of a stakeholder or group of stakeholders in your destination. In what ways do you think they need to improve their capacity in order to engage effectively with a pro-poor approach to tourism? How do you think their needs can be met?

Exercise 13 Who needs to play what role?

Prepare:

- Handout of table 5 (part 2, introduction) showing the seven mechanisms and the roles of different stakeholder groups in implementing them (work sheet 12).

Instruction:

- MDW: Work in pairs.

- SDW: Work in small groups.

Allocate **one** mechanism to each pair/group. Think of an example of how this mechanism might work in your destination. What would be required of each stakeholder group (enterprises/tourists/ tour operators/the poor)? How well placed is each group to deliver what is required? Do you think this is something that could happen?

Exercise 14 Which mechanisms to consider

Prepare:

- Handout 1 of the seven mechanisms (work sheet 13).

- Handout 2 of table 6 (part 2, introduction) showing a range of scenarios and suggesting for each the possible mechanisms to consider (work sheet 14).

Instruction:

- MDW: Work in pairs.

- SDW: Work in small groups.

Choose the situation that best describes your destination. Discuss how the particular mechanisms suggested might work there. Do you think that all the mechanisms suggested will work equally well in your destination? Can you think whether any of the other mechanisms might also work in your situation?

Exercise 15 Focus on first selected mechanism

Prepare:

* Handout with the case study boxes used in the manual to illustrate the selected mechanism.

Instruction:

* Work in pairs or small groups. Allocate a case study box to each pair/group. Identify three reasons why this is a good example of this mechanism. Can you see any weaknesses in this approach? Do you think that it could work in your destination? Bring your findings back to the whole group for discussion.

Exercise 16 Focus on second selected mechanism

* As exercise 15.

Exercise 17 Selecting indicators

Prepare:

* Handout with small selection of case studies from the manual

Instruction:

* Work in small groups. Choose one of the case studies and identify possible indicators and monitoring processes relevant to their situation. Who would need to be involved?